Westminster United Presbyterian Church
1501 WEST CLEVELAND RD.
SOUTH BEND, INDIANA 46628

Galilean Journey

D1056632

Virgil Elizondo

Galilean Journey

The Mexican-American Promise

ORBIS BOOKS

Maryknoll, New York 10545

The Catholic Foreign Mission Society of America (Maryknoll) recruits and trains people for overseas missionary service. Through Orbis Books Maryknoll aims to foster the international dialogue that is essential to mission. The books published, however, reflect the opinions of their authors and are not meant to represent the official position of the society.

This work is based on the author's doctoral dissertation *Mestissage, violence culturelle, annonce de l'évangile,* presented at the Institut Catholique, Paris, 1978.

Copyright © 1983 by Orbis Books, Maryknoll, NY 10545
All rights reserved
Manufactured in the United States of America

Manuscript editor: William E. Jerman

Library of Congress Cataloging in Publication Data

Elizondo, Virgilio P.
  Galilean Journey: The Mexican-American promise.

  "Based on the author's doctoral dissertation
Mestissage, violence culturelle, annonce de l'évangile,
presented at the Institut Catholique, Paris,
1978"—T.p. verso.
  Includes bibliographical references and index.
  1. Mexican Americans—Religion. 2. Catholic Church
—United States. 3. United States—Church history.
I. Title.
BX1407.M48E44   1983   208'.96872073   82-18852
ISBN 0-88344-151-9 (pbk.)

208.9
ELi

Westminster United Presbyterian Church
1501 WEST CLEVELAND RD.
SOUTH BEND, INDIANA 46628

To
the Peoples of Mexico and the United States of America

May God reward them for the good they have done
and have mercy on them for the evil they have done.
May we in turn learn to follow them in their good example
and not follow them in their bad example.

CONTENTS

PREFACE

This is a book that induces its reader to see familiar things in an unfamiliar light. We thought we understood, in general terms, the history, identity, religious affiliation, and human problems—conflicts—of the Mexican-American people. But Virgil Elizondo challenges us: "Is it really so? Are you sure?" And he goes beyond merely crumbling our certitudes. He does not ensconce himself at the level of analysis; he seeks to discover a path leading outward and upward. And he succeeds.

Elizondo points to a new frontier. It turns out to be not far distant. Culture—in the broad sense of the term—is a major part of his concern here. Every modern human culture that we know of is a composite. It is *mestizo,* made up of disparate elements, which nonetheless form an integrated whole. The cultural frontier is at the heart of every human grouping, every individual.

A human grouping—like any other living organism—cannot survive except by confronting the unknown, the unexpected. It must re-form its identity at the threshold of every new encounter. It is engaged in a ceaseless effort of absorption, assimilation, and transmutation—of symbols, images, modes of existence. To try to arrest this movement at any given point—whether from nostalgia over the past or the dream of a sirenic utopia—is to condemn it to sclerosis and death.

A culture is not a museum collection of objects and symbols; it is a permanent process of disintegration and reintegration. The culture of a given people is shaped by what it receives from its roots—but also by what confronts it from without. It is sustained by hope—and by contestation. Threatened by death every time it puts a foot forward, it pays a price for the privilege of continued life. As in the ancient Aztec rite, a living heart is sacrificed so that tomorrow the sun may shine.

There is an abundance of learned words and phrases available to describe much of the subject matter of this book. Such concepts as "minorities," "ethnic groups," "local cultures," and the like, fill many a volume resting on library shelves. Elizondo's purpose is not to add yet another treatise or theory to the ensemble. Rather, he aligns his particular purpose—to understand the dynamics that govern the life and death of an ethnic group, the Mexican-American, to be most specific—within the perspectives resulting from the myriads of studies made to date.

His approach gives the reader insights into such concepts as "races" and "minorities," for example. They presuppose an ideal norm—a "pure race," a "correct majority." But there is no such thing as a "pure race," any more than there ever was a "pure nation," a "pure state." This thinking took shape in a *historical* context; it can be dated. There was a time when Europe thought of itself as the center of the world. When Europeans set out to colonize the Americas—Britons in the north, Spaniards in the south—they brought this mentality with them.

It is still alive today. The notion of a "pure race" is far from dead. The hazy notion of a "center," in relation to which some human groups are "marginal" or "minor," is far from dead. Such thought-categories, buried *alive* in the collective memory, show up in diverse superstructures of society. They are not mere historical curios; they are principles of action and violence.

Besides physical, military, economic, and political violence, there is also such a thing as cultural violence. The (Spanish) *mestizo*, at the heart of this study, is an indication of it. *Mestizos*, offspring of two distinctive groups, find themselves rejected by both. They are recognized in terms of what they are not. The *mestizo* is someone who is *not*. Cultural violence goes far: it suppresses the *identity* of individuals and groups.

Human groups encounter one another—and attack one another. They dream and speak of harmony and freedom even as they kill and exploit one another.

It is still the European ideas of the Renaissance and Enlightenment that largely set the tone. Strengthened by the might of united world influences, they preside over war and peace. In the final analysis, it is the human being in the abstract, the *homo economicus* born in Europe centuries ago, who remains the norm. The West still imposes its concepts of identity, power, unity, morality, democracy—surprised when the words come back to it bathed in blood, even more copious than the blood that flowed from the altars of Tlatelolco and terrified the Spanish conquistadores.

Something is awry. The adventure of the world's closer unity, its meeting with itself, evidently bears within it the seeds of destruction. Can nothing better be expected?

It is not enough, however, to *analyze*. Elizondo's second originality lies in carrying his research beyond the point where many others have stopped: religion. Religion—Christianity, in this case—is an essential component of the Mexican-American *mestizaje*. Christianity provided partial motivation for the ventures of the conquistadores; it was also an instrument of domination, extermination—cultural violence. Can an instrument of oppression be an instrument of liberation? Can a religion that was imposed by violence be the vehicle to a richer identity?

For Latin America, the reversal took place through a symbol-image, that of Our Lady of Guadalupe—a kind of image that is itself marginal to traditional theological exploration. Elizondo brings out its coherence and validity, then and now, for it lives still in popular devotion. Identity is found not only in ideas or in written texts, but in the lived experience of a historically continuous group of believers, an arm of the people of God.

The experience of the people rings true. It transmits images, attitudes, expressions that—without the people's being clearly conscious of it—are a conduit of the mainstream of Christian tradition. There is a "saga"— incarnational folklore—of Jesus that is a spontaneous expression of popular faith.

From this starting point, a new reading of the gospels becomes possible. Not the least original aspect of Elizondo's study is his proposal for a cultural rereading of the gospels, and a gospel rereading of cultural dynamics. There is thus a mutual interaction between, on the one hand, group identity and group mission, and, on the other, the foundational events of Christian presence as recorded in the foundational documents, the sacred texts.

What do the Scriptures tell us about *mestizaje,* socio-cultural identity, political domination? In *those terms,* nothing at all, or very little at most. The Scriptures are not a manual of psychology or of social ethics. To want to use them as such is to doom oneself to artificial parallels, such as those of a Bossuet who tried to find a political system in the gospels, or of some contemporary theologians who too easily find their ideas, of extrabiblical provenance, verified in the scriptural texts.

But the gospel does touch on the concrete realities of everyday life. It displaces some "certainties" that we held and it projects other outlines. It makes us see things anew. Starting from *its* viewpoint, we can come *back* to our questions about *mestizaje,* identity, domination.

For centuries Christianity essentially saw itself as a closed triangle bordered by Europe, South and North America. And it was from within that triangle that modern world culture, by and large, came into existence. It is those frontiers that are being stretched today. The surmounting of boundaries is a prerequisite for world fellowship.

On this score, as on others, Elizondo, expressly treating a relatively small section of the earth's inhabited surface, points to solutions of global problems. His treatment of Mexican-American *mestizaje* leads naturally to thoughts about global *mestizaje.*

Elizondo's analysis and reflections point out to us certain major elements of a problem situation—and he points out a path, a way, to confront the problems. It is the way of the person of faith, who understands that the gospel and humankind were fathered by the same God. From this perspective, his book goes beyond theology. Or rather, it is an exercise in a new type of theology, a practical theology: word and instrument of human inspiration and transformation.

The writing of this Mexican-American man of thought and action has had a deep resonance in me, a European educator. He has obliged me to reexamine some of my thought-categories, and he has opened up unexplored vistas.

JACQUES AUDINET
Institut Catholique,
Paris

(Translated by Eva Fleischner)

INTRODUCTION

This work is the story of the universal human quest as lived and expressed by the Mexican-American people of the Southwest U.S.A. It is a study of the struggle for life, survival, identity, human dignity, equality, liberty, happiness.

Who are the Mexican-Americans? What is to become of them as a people? Will they melt away like other groups to emerge simply as "Mexican" on Mexican Independence Day or the feast of Our Lady of Guadalupe? Will they cease to exist as a people and be reduced to the pages of a colorful folklore that can be reenacted annually by some historical society? Will the ways of their ancestors be enshrined only in museums and works of art?

As Christians, we can pose even deeper questions. Does the gospel have something to offer at the crossroads between the death and life of a people? Does it have a place in the liberation movement of a people? Is there a relationship between the gospel and the cultural birth and evolution of a people? Does the gospel really make any difference? Does the gospel really bring life or is it more of a death mask?

It is my firm conviction that the identity and mission of the Mexican-American people will not only continue but will be purified, ennobled, and strengthened by the discovery of its fundamental identity and mission in its acceptance and following of Jesus of Nazareth as the Lord of history and life. His own history and that of the church that re-presents his salvific presence among us have shown that he can turn rejection into acceptance, ugliness into beauty, isolation into fellowship, sickness into health, death into life.

It is equally my conviction that we will never truly appreciate the full meaning and significance of Jesus as savior and liberator unless we are keenly aware of our own historical and existential situation. It is not only individuals as such but the totality of their life that is touched and transformed when Jesus is welcomed to be the Lord of history.

My own frame of reference is that of a native American citizen born of Mexican parents in San Antonio, Texas. In the neighborhood where I grew up, Spanish was the only language spoken. I learned English only when I went to school.

I am a Mexican-American, whose basic language and culture is the bilingual, bicultural reality of the Southwest U.S.A., the great frontier between Anglo and Latin America. I am a Roman Catholic by culture and by adult

1

free choice. I am a priest critical of both my church and my country, while loving them both as I do my own parents. It is from this optic that I search for the truth that has shaped my life to this point, and will shape my future.

The process that led to this book has been a lifelong process. It is my own story and that of my people; as such, it began long before my birth, and it ranges far beyond my personal experiences and aspirations. I speak from a lifetime of familiarity with Mexican-Americans, working with and listening to them especially in the years since the founding of the Mexican-American Cultural Center (MACC) in San Antonio, in 1971. I have worked, agonized, searched, laughed, cried, dreamed, joked, prayed, and celebrated with hundreds of thousands of fellow Mexican-Americans from Texas to Alaska, from California to New England, and—perhaps surprisingly to some—in Turkey, Germany, Iran. Our Mexican-American people is everywhere; and, as different as we are from one another, we are a distinct people, we have a common soul. *Somos un pueblo!*

The more we at MACC probed the questions facing our people, the more it became evident that we could not really know ourselves unless we became more conscious of our historical process. We did not think of it as simply *the past,* but as the roots still nourishing our contemporary identity.

One part of that historical process was deeply rooted in the ancient past of pre-Hispanic Mexico. Another was rooted in sixteenth-century Spain. Yet another came from the gospels—their cultural implantation in the life of the people. The fourth major influence—the most recent—came from our Anglo-American history. In the fascinating quest for the traces of these historico-cultural influences, I unearthed unsuspected treasures of the Mexican-American past still very much alive—and unsuspected—in contemporary life.

To American scholars and research workers, politicians and businessmen, educators and administrators, we remained—and remain—something of a mystery. We do not fit neatly into their judgment categories. They see us as a problem to be solved—somewhat like our language, our own amalgam of Spanish and English; it does not fit neatly into the categories of either "standard" Spanish or "standard" (North American) English. To language scientists, it is a problem. But not for us: we just imbibe it and speak it!

We have a soul of our own. To be made to the image and likeness of God does *not* require the finishing touches of Anglo-American melting-pot assimilation.

Besides my own family and fellow Mexican-Americans, others have played a significant role in my own formation and the development of this book. During my years of study at the East Asian Pastoral Institute in Manila, 1968 and 1969, I learned much about the beauty of cultural diversity in the world from Fr. Alfonso Nebreda. I also came to understand better, with his help, the deeply personal and personalizing nature of Christian revelation and faith. I came to realize better that, in the light of the *personal* character of the incarnation, the cultural conditioning of the individual was not to be thought of as just an aid to proclaim the gospel, but as the medium through which God chose to reveal himself.

Later I met Fr. Gustavo Gutiérrez of Lima, Peru. He was to influence me deeply. What I had already sensed implicitly was reinforced, clarified, and developed by Gustavo. Every concrete Christian community had the privilege and obligation to reflect on the meaning of its faith. No matter how many excellent christologies there might be in the world, it was no excuse for the local community not to work out its own expression of who Christ is and what he is doing in their midst.

And it was precisely the *marginated* of every socio-political group who were in the privileged position of being most closely similar to the poor at the time of Christ. They were the first ones to hear his word, to be converted to him and his way, and to begin preaching a new alternative to the world.

Another person to become a very close friend and companion was Fr. John Linskens. He deepened my love for the word of God, especially the New Testament. I met him in Manila and later was able to invite him to San Antonio to work with us at MACC. Without his help I would never have learned how to reread the New Testament in such a way as to be able to translate it into the living language of the people.

Finally, there is Jacques Audinet, professor at the Catholic Institute, Paris. In 1968, on a flight from Medellín to Miami, he made me aware of the unsuspected wealth hidden in the reality of *mestizaje*. When I began to think about, it turned all my previous thinking inside out. Jacques later invited me to go to Paris, to turn the raw material of my six years of pastoral work into a doctoral dissertation in theology.[1] During my year in Paris, 1976–1977, Jacques became my closest friend—and my most severe critic. Often I asked him to tell me how he wanted me to shape my work, but he refused. It was to be *my* work. He was out to liberate me! He did not want me simply to imitate him and his ways. To him—teacher, father, friend, brother—*¡muchísimas gracias!*

I will always be indebted to the many other persons in all the places where I have had the privilege of living and working. In particular, in the development of this book, I must thank my other professors and friends in Paris: M. D. Chenu, OP, Claude Geffré, OP, Christian Duquoc, OP, Charles Kannengieser, SJ, Michael Aubineau, SJ, Abel Pasquier, Regine de Charlat, José María Eguia, SJ, and all the Jesuits of the Rue de Grenelle residence; without them I would never have completed this project.

A special word of thanks too to the entire team at the MACC: Ricardo Ramirez, Dorothy Folliard, Ruben Alfaro, Angela Erevia, Juan Alfaro, Leonard Anguiano, Loyola Mestas, Dolorita Martinez, and Marcene Klemm. Much of them is in these pages. Without their help, I would still be working on the first draft of this manuscript. My own archbishop and close friend, Patrick Flores, was a very special source of inspiration and encouragement and Bishop R. Peña of El Paso who has always been a close friend and supporter.

Thanks too to Ricky Flores who helped me to revise the final manuscript so as to incorporate the suggestions of my doctoral committee, my friends, and the publisher. And thanks to William E. Jerman for his part in editing the dissertation text for publication in book form.

PART ONE

The Mexican-American Experience

Contemporary Mexican-Americans can trace their origins to two great invasions and conquests: the Spanish and the Anglo-American. Both conquests ushered in an era of colonization, oppression, and exploitation. But the confrontation of parent cultures also produced a new ethnos, a new people: the Spanish–Indian confrontation gave birth to the Mexican people; the Anglo-American—Mexican confrontation gave birth to the Mexican-American people.

French biologist J. Ruffie maintains that from the birth of Europe, thirty-five thousand years ago, when the invading Cromagnons integrated with the indigenous Neanderthals, no ethnogenetic event of similar magnitude took place until the birth of Mexico, less than five hundred years ago.[1] I am of the opinion that a similar event of at least equal magnitude has already begun to take place in the Southwest of the United States of America—an area larger than Western Europe and populated by some thirty-five million persons.

The word we shall be using in this book to designate the origination of a new people from two ethnically disparate parent peoples is the Spanish word *mestizaje* (from *mestizo,* "mixed," "hybrid"). The suffering involved in, but also the positive potential represented by, the twofold Mexican-American *mestizaje* can be appreciated only against the background of the European mentality prevalent at the time of the European conquest and colonization of the Americas. It has conditioned human relations, in the Western world and beyond, ever since.

Chapter 1

MESTIZAJE

1492: Year of Historic Beginnings

The year 1492 marked the emergence of three major changes affecting the whole course of subsequent Western history.

The last of the Crusades came to an end on January 2 of that year. Bells and Te Deum's sang out in jubilation throughout Europe. The "infidels" had finally been driven from the soil of Christian Europe. Catholic Spain finally concluded its eight hundred-year war with the Arabs, expelling them from the last corner of the Iberian peninsula. For the first time in its history, Spain was a free and politically united kingdom.

In March of that year the first religiously inspired racial legislation was passed in Europe. The Spanish law decreed that the Jews, guilty of the crime of deicide, could not remain in Spain. Those who did not convert to Christianity were expelled. Many were massacred when they fled to Africa. Those who converted were never considered to be *fully* Christian: the stain of deicide was too deep even for the sacramental waters of baptism. Jews would be handed over to the Inquisition on the flimsiest pretexts of heresy; they would be shunned and harassed for centuries.

The third historic event took place in October of that year when Christopher Columbus "discovered" the New World—the lands that had been discovered thousands of years earlier by Asian and Polynesian migrants and seafarers. The aftermath of Columbus's discovery entailed massive and irreversible world changes far deeper than merely a change in political boundaries or economic systems. The great European conquest and expansion westward had begun.

The conquest of the bronze peoples inhabiting the Americas and the subsequent wholesale uprooting and enslavement of hundreds of thousands of black Africans by white Europeans would engender and consolidate a racist[1] mentality unprecedented in world history. As masses of persons were slaughtered or condemned to a life of abject misery and menial labor for the enrichment of others, a mentality justifying the inhuman treatment was built up, justifying the outrages and social despoliation of entire peoples.

Europeans had been battling one another, or off on Crusades, for centu-

7

ries. Life in Europe was largely a matter of poverty and harshness for the overwhelming majority of the population. The "good life" was reserved to a very small percentage of the overall population—the titled nobility and landowners, their courtiers and clergy.

But then a new "humanism" emerged, bringing with it great enthusiasm and great expectations. The discovery of vast new lands gave Europeans a new lease on life. Undreamed-of opportunities were suddenly revealed. Everyone would now be able to make a name for themselves. The end of feudalism marked the inauguration of the individual. Inheritance was no longer the only route to aristocracy: virtually anyone could accumulate a fortune!

Europe was intoxicated with the prospects of wealth from the New World that seemed to be waiting for them to reach out and pluck. But what would be a new life of freedom, opportunity, advancement, and wealth for the Europeans would be the beginning of enslavement, decimation, isolation, and dehumanization for others. The human sacrifices offered to "nature gods" scandalized the Europeans, but they would not hesitate to offer Indians and blacks to the gods of profit and greed.

A number of key factors coalesced to foster and cement European hegemony over the rest of the world. The newly discovered power of ocean-going ships and advanced weaponry gave them a mobility and fighting power far superior to what was available in Africa and the Americas. The motivational power of the new individualism provided the personal impetus for European adventurers to make a name for themselves. Power and might came to be equated with success and righteousness.

The industrial revolution and capitalism would bring with them new needs for raw materials, cheap labor, and manipulative schemes. The printing press and the Enlightenment provoked a culturo-intellectual stirring and the promulgation of the idea of a "universal person"—who had to be a universal *man,* in that age—pure and normative for all humankind. The way that universal man looked, ate, drank, spoke, acted, thought, wrote, dressed, lived, and prayed would be transmitted to the world at large as normative for all. Those not measuring up to that image would be considered underdeveloped, inferior. The conviction that Christianity was the only true and absolute way to God only added fuel to the determination to conquer and dominate the whole world.

The three historic changes of 1492 launched an era of violence such as the world had not known before. Violence itself was nothing new to the world, but the extent and depth of the dehumanization stemming from 1492 was, and remains, without parallel. It is still operative today in the poverty, oppression, and degradation of Indians, blacks, and others in "undecolonialized" parts of the world.

European culture took on new racial characteristics. Europe saw its own culture as the epitome of human achievement; it saw its religion as the only true religion. Anything else was inferior—uncivilized and false. The step from ethnocentrism to racism was an easy and even "logical" one: peoples are inferior because nature made them that way.

It was at that time that the concept of humankind—the *one* human "race"—was broken down into a multiplicity of races, with color as the major determinant of race. Divisions among peoples on the basis of color would be considered *absolute* differences: different colors meant different races—different degrees on a descending scale of humanness.

The old, regional, antagonistic European ethnocentrisms found a new unity in sealing a rigid frontier between the white European "race" and the "other races" of the world. Europocentrism became part of the inner culture of the European peoples. It formed an unquestioned assumption permeating all levels of human existence—religious, political, philosophical, educational, economic, military, literary. "We alone are fully human" became the basic cultural dogma of the European personality.

European men of science and letters tried to explain the otherness of the peoples of other continents, not by asking *them* who they were, but by contrasting them to themselves. When Columbus arrived in the New World, the peoples living there were not asked who they were; they were simply called *Indios*—inhabitants of India—and we have lived with that colossal, egocentric mistake ever since.

It was not from evil intentions as such, but from the confluence of a multiplicity of historical factors that racism came to be systematized and ingrained. Europeans, because of their rapid discoveries, conquests, and overseas expansion, easily developed the conviction that they were superior—and the others were inferior. From this came the rationalization, legitimation, institutionalization, and perpetuation of the violence of racism.

The "golden age of reason" was well named: gold could buy reason, could buy science, and science, through the chemistry of rational manipulation, could turn subjective prejudice into "proven scientific theorem." Who would dispute science? The division of humankind into superior and inferior races was "scientifically established." And it is still with us.

First Mestizaje:
The Spanish-Catholic Conquest of Mexico

The Catholic conquest and colonization of the southern American hemisphere differed radically from the Protestant conquest and colonization of North America.

The Spaniards were not as such concerned about the salvation of their own souls: that, for them, was taken for granted. But there was concern among them for the salvation of the peoples they discovered in the New World.

Furthermore, the conquistadores and their troops were men of their time, for whom sexual relations were as "natural" as breathing or eating.

Westminster Presbyterian Church
1501 WEST CLEVELAND RD.
SOUTH BEND, INDIANA 46628

They were just as racist and superior-minded as other Europeans, but they were not racial purists. From the beginning, the Spaniards mixed freely with the indigenous population, taking women as bed-partners, concubines, or even as wives. Whether their children were legitimate or illegitimate made little difference to them: they gave them their names and claimed them as their own. Racial mixing was not discouraged by the Catholic kings of Spain or by the Vatican.[2]

Thus the Catholic conquest of the Americas brought with it a new people, a new ethnos—*la raza mestiza* ("mixed clan, family," or "race"). This was truly the *new American people,* for it was born together with the birth of the Americas. The indigenes were pre-Americans and the immigrants were Europeans. The people that arose from their encounter was the fully new American people—*los Americanos.*

The birth process of Mexico-America can be dated back to Good Friday, April 22, 1519, the day when Hernando Cortez arrived in Mexico. It is difficult for a non-Mexican and even for Mexicans themselves to fathom the full impact and significance of the historical process that began with the violent meeting of those two powers, Spain and Mexico. It was the first war between the two worlds they represented.

Mestizaje—the birth of a new people from two preexistent peoples— *could* come about in various ways. But de facto it has most often come about through military conquest, colonization, and religious imposition. This certainly was the case in the Spanish-Indian *mestizaje.*

Conquest comes through military power, motivated by economic interests. But once military conquest takes place, it easily proceeds to *total* conquest. It imposes not only the institutions of the conqueror but a new worldview, a basic philosophy of life. The new worldview disrupts the worldview of the conquered to such an extent that their ways no longer make sense. The ideas, logic, art, customs, language, and religion of the conqueror are forced into the life of the conquered. Even if they resist, the ways of the powerful begin to penetrate their minds and their lifestyle, so that even when political and economic independence are gained at a later stage, the indigenous culture can never again return to its preconquest patterns.

Beneath the violence of physical conquest there is the deeper violence of the disruption that destroys the conquereds' worldview, which gave cohesion and meaning to their existence. The deepest part of that worldview is the bedrock of the fundamental religious symbols, providing the ultimate rootage of the group's self-identity: the symbols that mediate the absolute. They are the ultimate tangible expressions of the anchoring of the relativity of the worldview in the absolute of divinity. Religious symbols are the final justification of the group's worldview and the force that cements all the elements of a group's life into a cohesive, meaningful world order.

Hence the introduction of new religious symbols, especially when they are the symbols of a dominant group, is in effect the ultimate violence. With nonviolent intentions, Catholic missionaries were the agents of a violence more radical than physical violence. They attempted to destroy what physical violence could not touch: the soul of the indigenous people. Despite the missionaries' opposition to the cruel and bloody ways of the conquistadores, the introduction of the religious symbols of the Spanish intruders in effect affirmed and justified the way of the powerful and discredited the way of the powerless at the deepest level of their existence.

Mother of the New Race

In 1531, ten years after the Spanish conquest of Indian Mexico, a mysterious event took place that was to have monumental and long-lasting effects. There is no scientific proof or disproof, or explanation, of the "apparition" of Our Lady of Guadalupe, but there can be no denying its impact on the Mexican people from that time to the present. Its inner meaning has been recorded in the collective memory of the people.

According to the legend, as Juan Diego, a Christian Indian of common status, was going from his home in the *barriada* ("district") near Tepeyac, a hill northwest of Mexico City, he suddenly heard beautiful music. As he approached the source of the music, a lady appeared to him. Speaking in Nahuatl, the language of the conquered, she ordered Juan Diego to go to the palace of the archbishop of Mexico, at Tlatelolco, and tell him that the Virgin Mary, "Mother of the true God through whom one lives," wanted a temple to be built on that site so that in it she could "communicate all her love, compassion, help, and defense to all the inhabitants of this land . . . to hear their lamentations and remedy their miseries, pain, and suffering."

After two unsuccessful attempts by Juan Diego to convince the bishop of the Lady's authenticity, the Virgin wrought a miracle. She sent Juan Diego to pick roses in a place where only desert plants grew. She then arranged the roses in his cloak and sent him to the bishop with the sign he had demanded. As Juan Diego unfolded his cloak in the presence of the bishop, the roses fell to the floor and the painted image of the Lady appeared on his cloak.[3]

The subjugated Mexican people came to life again because of Guadalupe. The response of the Indians was a spontaneous explosion of pilgrimages, festivals, and conversions to the religion of the Virgin. Out of their meaningless and chaotic existence of the postconquest years, a new meaning had erupted.

The real miracle was not the apparition but what happened to the defeated Indian. In the person of Juan Diego was represented the Indian nations defeated and slaughtered, but now brought to life. They who had been robbed of their lands and of their way of life and even of their gods were now coming to life. They who had been silenced were now speaking again through the voice of the Lady. They who wanted only to die now wanted to live.

As at Bethlehem when the Son of God was born as Jesus and signaled the reversal of the power of the Roman empire, so at Tepeyac Christ set foot on the soil of the Americas and signaled the reversal of European domination. Tepeyac symbolized the birth of the Mexican people and the birth of Mexican Christianity. They were no longer an orphaned people and the new religion was no longer that of foreign gods.

The power of hope offered by the drama of Guadalupe came from the fact that the unexpected good news of God's presence was offered to all by someone from whom nothing special was expected: the conquered Indian, the lowest of the low. Conversion begins with the poor and marginated; they are the heralds, the prophets, of a new humanity.

The new people of the land would now be the *pueblo mestizo, la raza mestiza*. And the new Christianity would be neither a cultural expression of Iberian Catholicism nor a mere continuation of the preconquest religions of the indigenous peoples, but a new incarnation of Christianity in and of the Americas.

In *la Morenita* ("the brown Lady") the orphaned and illegitimate Mexican people discovered their true and legitimate mother. "We are not the children of a violated woman, but children of the unsoiled Virgin Mother. In Guadalupe we pass from the shame and degradation of illegitimacy to the grandeur and pride of being *pure Mexican*."

The events of 1531 marked only the beginning of what would take centuries to accomplish: self-dignity, equality, freedom, an identity to be proud of. But it *was* the all-important beginning.

The symbolism of *la Morenita* opened up a new possibility for racio-cultural dialogue and exchange. The synthesis of the religious iconography of the Spanish with that of the indigenous Mexican peoples into a single, coherent symbol-image ushered in a new, shared experience. The missioners and the people now had an authentic basis for dialogue. What the missioners had been praying for had now come in an unexpected (and for some, unwanted) way.

The cultural clash of sixteenth-century Spain and Mexico was resolved and reconciled in the brown Lady of Guadalupe. In her the new *mestizo* people finds its meaning, its uniqueness, its unity. Guadalupe is the key to understanding the Christianity of the New World, the self-image of Mexicans, of Mexican-Americans, and of all Latin Americans.

If anthropologically Latin America is a new *mestizo* people, socio-politically it is still the European conquistadores and their descendants who are in control. Local oligarchies have replaced kings and their viceroys, but the hierarchical structures of society have remained virtually intact. The labels affixed to social strata are the same. Wealth, ownership, color, name, language, and education are still the primary determinants of personal status in the racio-classist structures of Latin American society.

Some Latin Americans say that they never experienced racism until they came to the United States. But dark-skinned Latin Americans will tell you of many ways in which racism is the "law of the land" in Latin America. See for yourself what roles are assigned to the dark-skinned and light-skinned in Latin American television plays and movies.

While the masses are starving physically and culturally, the ultra-rich minorities of Latin America are squandering their lives in overindulgence and general debauchery. Very superior-minded, they appear to have no sense of social responsibility. Convinced of their own superiority, they simply take it for granted that the masses owe them their good life. They are outraged when the poor begin to learn how to read and write. They are stupefied when the faceless and nameless begin to talk about their human dignity and their human rights. They are shocked when rural workers make efforts to organize themselves and begin talking about fair wages, decent housing, and education. *"¡Igualados! ¡No conocen su lugar!"* ("They make themselves out to be equal! They don't know their place!").

Only in Our Lady of Guadalupe, the common mother of all the inhabitants of Latin America, is the rigid dichotomy of the *"we* versus *they"* mentality overcome in the eruption of a new and renovative alternative. As time goes on, it will be through the common recognition of her common motherhood that the various divided ethnic groups in Latin America will be able to move to the experience of a new *us*. From many peoples, a new *raza* is in the process of being born. *"No somos ni españoles, ni criollos, ni indios, . . . somos* puro mexicanos, . . . *el pueblo mexicano que es el Mexico de hoy"* ("We are neither Spanish nor Creole nor Indians; we are *pure Mexicans*, the Mexican people which is the Mexico of today.").[4]

Second Mestizaje:
The Nordic-Protestant Conquest of Mexico

The Protestant colonization of North America can be characterized, in general terms, as the transplantation of North Europeans to a new land. They conquered, colonized, and cleared the land of the indigenous inhabitants. Their own religious salvation was important to them, but not so much that of the natives. Church affiliation became a thing of importance, but evangelization was hardly attempted.

The Europeans came seeking religious freedom and a better life for themselves. Racially, they were purist in their thinking and abhorred the idea of miscegenation. Laws were quickly passed in the original colonies prohibiting all types of racial mixture between the European immigrants and the indigenes. A new Anglo-Saxon Europe was what they wanted, not a new ethnos, a new genetic people.

Settlers rejoiced to find that God had been pleased to send a "wonderful plague" among the savages, so as to free the land for "civilized occupation."[5] The Protestant colonizers saw themselves engaged in a divinely inspired enterprise: eliminating the "savages" was equivalent to ridding the land of sin and Satan. The building of the new nation with its systematic elimination of the native population and its importation of black slaves took on the trappings and sanctions of a religious enterprise.[6]

The European colonizers made rapid progress. Political independence from Europe came much sooner than for Latin American nations. The new nation was to be the new Israel, the new Athens, the new Rome, and the new Jerusalem all in one. God had providentially chosen them to carry the new world order to the rest of humanity, which still "lived in the darkness of savagery and sin." Commercial ventures demanded new lands and Manifest Destiny justified the great westward expansion. Conquest, power, and wealth were the evident signs of God's election. Poverty and misery were signs of sinfulness and rejection.

A presupposed equality among the English-speaking whites was the basis for the new society, with its participatory and democratic forms of government. Everyone (if white) had an equal chance to make someone of themselves. Results were what counted; the ways to success were seldom scrutinized or questioned.

Anglo-Saxon Americans always had a deep sense of ownership and liberty. They had a good self-image and a strong feeling of superiority over other ethnic groupings. Their own giant strides in the birth and development of the young nation "proved" it to them.

With such deep-rooted convictions of a divinely decreed superiority, it cannot be surprising that Protestant American expansionism would collide with the Catholic colonial empire to the southwest of it. Manifest Destiny demanded its elimination in favor of "progress" and an end to idolatrous papism and degenerate Spanish ways.

Elizabeth and Cromwell had already established a policy that stealing from Catholic Spain was a noble endeavor in favor of liberation and civilization. Successful pirates were honored and knighted for their deeds. Piracy against Spain was part of the Anglo-American legacy that gave a religious and patriotic incentive to excursions against Mexico.

Anglo-Americans started to move into the northern territories of what was then Mexican territory. Some came legally, but most were illegal immigrants who had no regard for Mexican laws.

From the very first encounters, the Anglo-American immigrants looked upon the Mexicans (for them, all the Spanish-speaking) with disdain. The Mexican was brown, *mestizo,* Spanish-speaking, Roman Catholic. The North American was white, pure-blooded (racial admixture was contamination), English-speaking, Protestant. And the Mexican had a totally different worldview from that of the aggressive, land-hungry, power-intoxicated Anglo-American Indian-fighter.[7] The Mexicans were labeled inferior, lazy, deceitful, superstitious, incapable of assimilation.

The Anglo-Americans never willingly submitted to Mexican rule, even though they had accepted the hospitality and generosity of the Mexican government. There were early attempts to win independence from Mexico. However, it was not until the unpopular government of Santa Ana, coupled with mounting Anglo-American independence sentiments throughout

Texas, that the first war for independence from Mexico was started, in 1836.

In 1845 the French *Journal des Débats* published an article describing President James Polk's "lust for power and conquest."[8] It stated that the conquest of Texas would be but the first step toward the conquest of Mexico and eventually the entire American continent. In his inaugural address (March 4, 1845) Polk had stated:

> Foreign powers do not seem to appreciate the true character of our government. Our Union is a confederation of independent states, whose policy is peace with each other and all the world. To enlarge its limits is to extend the dominions of peace over additional territories and increasing millions.

In May 1846 the president of the United States declared war on Mexico. In his war message to the American congress, Polk stated that Mexico "has invaded our territory and shed American blood upon the American soil." That was his version of the hostilities that took place when he sent American troops into Mexican settlements on the southern bank of the Rio Grande.[9]

In January 1847 General Winfield Scott landed near Vera Cruz with ten thousand troops. Mexico itself was still divided by internal strife and its leaders were mistrustful of one another. Some Mexican states were not sure of the intentions of others and they refused to provide troops for defense against the invaders. Most of the Mexican army consisted of poorly motivated and ill-trained Indian conscripts.

Within six months the American army marched from Vera Cruz to Mexico City. On September 14 it occupied the Mexican capital. Negotiations were begun for a peace treaty. On February 2, 1848, the treaty was signed in the village of Guadalupe-Hidalgo.

For the general American population, the time of war with Mexico had been a time of historico-cultural unity, national identity, optimism, self-assurance, and self-righteousness. The Anglo-Americans had won the war of 1812, had developed a national spirit, were anxious to expand.

Mexico, on the other hand, was just emerging from three hundred years of colonial rule. Its population was not a coherent group of transplanted Europeans with a common historico-cultural memory; it was a vast mixture of indigenous peoples—speaking diverse languages—*mestizos,* and Europeans, all enjoying equal citizenship under the law.

Under the terms of the Guadalupe-Hidalgo treaty, Mexico ceded to the United States a vast territory including the present states of California, Arizona, and New Mexico, and large sections of Colorado, Nevada, and Utah. It also approved the prior annexation of Texas. The territory ceded to the United States was approximately half the size of prewar Mexico. In

return, the United States paid Mexico $15 million and guaranteed the prop-
erty rights and political rights of the "native" population. The conquered
Spanish-speaking people was guaranteed the right to retain its cultural au-
tonomy, its language, its religion, and traditions. How thoroughly these
provisions have been ignored is evident in the subsequent history of the
Southwest.

Since 1848 there has been a nearly unbroken history of direct and indirect, spontaneous and institutionalized, violence throughout the West and
Southwest. Leading institutions, both public and private, secular and religious, have adopted prejudicial attitudes and practices in regard to the
Mexican-American population. There is an abundance of well documented
cases of the most inhuman types of discrimination in schools, churches,
work places, social agencies, law-enforcement agencies—even cemeteries.[10]
Nor is this just past history; it is still prevalent.

Mexican-Americans, encountering suppression on every side, began to
think of themselves as inferior. Their ancient pride languished. It seemed to
many of them that the only way to be free human beings was to become like
the Anglo society—to forget their past and become as purely Anglo as possible.

The Guadalupe-Hidalgo treaty established a political border between the
two nations, but it could not establish a cultural or geographical boundary.
The frontier region continued to be a homogeneous region. Mexican citizens would continue to cross the political border without any thought of
entering a foreign country. Until recent years, Mexican citizens would come
and go over that border with the same nonchalance with which they would
cross a city street. The *familia* would come, not to a "foreign nation," but
simply to "the other stretch of the family property"—*"Vamos pa'l otro
lado."*

Conditions on both sides of the border encouraged Mexican migration:
Mexico had a surplus of unemployed workers, and growing U.S. industry
needed laborers. Poor Mexicans were accustomed to a peonage system; they
made good, subservient, reliable workers.

The Dynamics of Mestizaje

As a biological phenomenon, *mestizaje*—the generation of a new people
from two disparate parent peoples—has been very common in the evolution
of humankind. Scientists are of the opinion that there are few, if any, truly
"pure" ethnic groups left in the world. And "pure" or "purer" groups tend
to be weaker, because their genetic pool has been gradually drained. By
admixture, new human groups emerge and genetic make-up is strengthened.[11]

A new ethnic group will have *cultural,* as well as *biological,*
characteristics—a fact of history. And it will be welcomed or rejected by

established groups on the basis of the stereotypes that established groups have of themselves and of others.

Survival of the fittest appears to be the first (physico-cultural) law of society and of individuals. We struggle to protect ourselves against each other and to conquer others before they conquer us. We prepare for security by preparing for war. Only violent means seem able to control or curb violence. Might becomes right because power establishes its views as the objective norm to consolidate and justify its own achievements, its own position of privilege.

From this struggle for survival at the cost of others certain anthropologico-sociological characteristics and behavioral laws appear. Members of a dominant group see themselves as superior, pure, dignified, well developed, civilized. They see their "natural superiority" as the source of their superior achievements.

They look upon the conquered and colonized as inferior, impure, undignified, underdeveloped, uncivilized. The conquered are told that they must abandon their backward ways if they are to advance and become "humanized." Acculturation—accommodation—to the way of the dominant is equated with *human* development and progress.

Even the well intentioned among the dominant group find it very difficult to accept fully the other as other. Even though they may put themselves at their service and truly love them, there is still an inner rejection of their otherness. The "law" that the ways of the powerful, the established, are the norm for all is so deeply engrained that it takes a kind of dying to oneself to be able to break through the cultural enslavements that keep the dominant from appreciating the inner beauty, the values, the wisdom, the worth and dignity of a subjugated people.

In analyzing the dynamics between an oppressor in-group and an oppressed out-group, three constants appear so regularly through the course of history that they can be taken as *anthropological laws of human behavior.*

The tendency of *group inclusion/exclusion* seems to be a fundamental law of human nature. A dominant group will struggle to defend the characteristics of its own self-definition when threatened by disparate values seen as characteristics of another group. Weaker or dominated groups likewise fear and resist any type of intrusion. "Group purity" seems to be perceived as a basic, unquestioned, essential need that must be maintained. Tangible hallmarks—race, class, language, family name, education, economic status, social position, religion—are used to distinguish "us" from "them."

The second tendency that seems to be an anthropological law of human nature is that of *social distance*—at the individual, personal level (as distinguished from "group exclusivity"). Even when deep personal friendships or love relationships develop, social barriers interfere with harmonization. The deeply imbedded relationship of "superior/inferior" keeps individuals from truly and fully appreciating each other as equal.

"Paternalism" seems an example of this law—for example, when members of a dominant group sincerely reach out to help those who are in some way underprivileged, but—even unconsciously—make sure that the "superior/inferior" relationship is not altered. Or when the "help" they offer amounts to making it easier for an out-group to assimilate itself to the in-group.

The third constant—or anthropological law of human nature—is that anyone who threatens to diminish or destroy the barriers of group separation must be eliminated.

Mestizaje is feared by established groups because it is perceived as a threat to the barriers of separation that consolidate self-identity and security. It is perceived as a threat to the security of human belonging—that is, to the inherited cultural identity that clearly defines who I am to myself and to the world.

A *mestizo* group represents a particularly serious threat to its two parent cultures. The *mestizo* does not fit conveniently into the analysis categories used by either parent group. The *mestizo* may understand them far better than they understand him or her. To be an insider-outsider, as is the *mestizo,* is to have closeness to and distance from both parent cultures. A *mestizo* people can see and appreciate characteristics in its parent cultures that they see neither in themselves nor in each other. It is threatening to be in the presence of someone who knows us better than we know ourselves.

The potential for regeneration inherent in a *mestizo* group will not come to fruition by itself. A *mestizo* group can simply assimilate itself to one of its parent groups, and continue doing unto others as has been done unto it. Inasmuch as partial assimilation is by nature and nurture already inculcated into the *mestizo* group, the seeds of this tendency have been planted.

The path of living out the radical meaning and potential of a *mestizo* regeneration will be much more difficult. Will the Mexican-American people simply revert to the ways of the parent group or will it lead the way to a new creation? That is a question I cannot answer; I can only point toward its possibility, the richness that it could bring to all, and the role that the Christian faith plays here, by way of illustration and animation.

Chapter 2

FROM CULTURAL BIRTH TO MATURITY

The Mexican-American People

February 2, 1848, marked the culmination of a long series of events leading to the end of one era and the beginning of another—the birth of a new people. Mexican-Americans were not simply "Mexicans living in the United States." As a distinct people, they were, and are, an autonomous variant of both Mexican and United States history. They are not simply a "compound"of the two, but the issue of a unique historical process that included aspects of both but with an originality of its own—the uniqueness of a newborn ethnic strain.

The Mexican-American historical odyssey can be seen as a passage through three phases. There was first the era of "survival efforts." Its cornucopia of frustrations led to a period of "development efforts," when Mexican-Americans tried to become "good Americans." Laying aside their own heritage, many of them tried to become full-fledged Anglo-Americans. The third phase was that of the *movimientos de liberación* ("liberation movements").

The dominant society had been telling them that *they* were the problem. But *they* began to ask whether there were even deeper problems within the dominant society. The Mexican-Americans had been told by others who they were; they had not searched their own past to discover for themselves who they were. Many finally reached the point of no longer wanting to be "like the others"—whether Mexican or American. Like the adolescent beginning to reach maturity, they did not want to be "copies" of either of their parents: they wanted to be(come) themselves.

The liberation movements, beginning in the 1960s, started to question the socio-cultural reality of their environment. They began to dig into their past, to penetrate to the development and meaning of their historical process. If not much had been written about it, there were other sources. In the absence of written history, oral history assumed greater importance. Their Mexican-American *cuentas, leyendas, y corridos* ("narratives, leg-

19

ends, and stories"), their art, poetry, and dances, kept their history alive, as seen and experienced by themselves—in *la visión de los vencidos* ("the vision of the conquered").

"Who are we?" they asked themselves. And they began to search for their roots—not in order to go backward, but in order to go forward. Just as the rediscovery of its Greco-Roman origins had brought a new vitality to Europe, so too the Mexican-Americans realized that they had to rediscover their origins in order to appreciate and celebrate their historical process, their true existential identity.

The Mexican-Americans had evolved through a specific social process, in a specific geographical region, in a specific period of time. Many of them in the earlier "development" phase of their evolution deliberately looked away from the painful foundational moment of their history. But the liberation movements saw it as the only starting point. They knew they had to be able to *celebrate* it as one of the key moments in their historical continuity—their growth and maturation as a unique human group within the overall history of humankind.

Identity

A Group Doubly Marginated and Rejected

The question asked Mexican-Americans over and over again is: "Are you American? Are you Mexican? Just what are you?" And if they are not *asked* to answer a question framed in preconceived terms, they are *told* over and over again who they are: Mexicans, Spicks, Chicanos, Hispanics, Latinos, greasers, beaners, wetbacks. . . .

But ask *Mexican-Americans* "Who are you?" in absolute terms—and you will get a variety of answers.

In my travels around the U.S.A., visiting Mexican-American communities, as also in workshops held at the Mexican-American Cultural Center, San Antonio, Texas, and elsewhere, at meetings on racio-cultural problems, I have met with thousands of Mexican-Americans at every level of educational, economic, political, and religious belonging. We immediately identify with one another as *Mestizo Norte-Americanos.* When Mexican-Americans meet, even for the first time, a direct personal bond is spontaneously experienced. But as soon as a "group name" is suggested— *Mexicano,* Mexican-American, Chicano—there is opposition, a flurry of objections.

In the replies to a questionnaire I sent out to leaders and members of Mexican-American communities, two significant trends were evident.

The first is that Mexican-Americans are divided between three choices as to the most appropriate name for the ethnic group: Chicano, *Mexicano,* or Mexican-American. Does this mean that there are at least three distinguishable subgroups, or are the names taken to refer to three diverse moments or aspects of the group's historical identity?

Generally speaking, it appears that those who prefer to call themselves *Mexicanos* still speak Spanish and maintain strong ties with old Mexico. Those who prefer to call themselves Mexican-Americans usually "accept" their Mexican heritage, but linguistically, socially, and culturally they identify more with the U.S. mentality and lifestyle. Those who prefer to be called Chicanos are those who are struggling to emerge with a new identity.

The second trend was that many answered in terms, not of proper names, but of—at first appearance—indeterminate or undefined names: *la raza, nuestra gente, mi gente* ("the clan or race, our people, my people"). Does this point to an *emerging* identity as yet resistive to fixation and more precise naming? Is it indicative of an *underlying security* coupled with an *insecurity* as to future growth and change, as yet not known with clarity? Is its apparent weakness a source and indication of strength? Does it indicate a definable ethnic group as yet *in the process of being born?*

My working hypothesis is that the answer to these questions is a definite *yes*. We are *la raza, el pueblo, la gente*. We are a *movement;* we are not a *monument*. We recognize one another; there is a bond, a sense of *familia,* that we all experience, but there is also an area of self-identity that we do not agree on.

There may be something to be learned by starting with what Mexican-Americans are *not*. They are not Mexicans from Mexico. Whether they are indigenous to the Southwest (many are) or have been born or brought up in other parts of the U.S.A., there is a continuity with their Mexican past, but there are also cultural and linguistic differences. In Mexico they are not accepted as "regular" Mexicans. They are referred to contemptuously as *pochos* (derivation uncertain; the meaning is "hollow but puffed up"; rotten fruit is said to be *pocho*) or *agringados* (from *a*—"to, toward, into"—*gringo*—a contemptuous or comical Latin American name for a North American, ultimately from the Spanish word for someone or something Greek, *griego,* typifying foreignness, as in the English phrase "it's all Greek to me!"—and *-ado*—a past-participial form indicating "made," or "done"; an *agringado* is a Latin American made into a "Yankee"). Their Spanish is ridiculed and they are considered inferior.

Nor have they been accepted within North American society. Young Mexican-Americans have been "good enough" to be taken into the U.S. military forces and even die in battle, but not good enough to be buried at home in the local cemetery. The *American GI Forum,* a Latino veterans' organization, claims that Mexican-Americans have won more Medals of Honor than any other ethnic group. Sgt. Jimmy Lopez, a Mexican-American marine from Globe, Arizona, one of the fifty-two American hostages held in Teheran, was one of the genuine heroes to emerge from that deplorable experience.[1]

Mexican-Americans have been considered second-class citizens, at best. One of the most painful, two-pronged "compliments" for them is when someone says, "For a Mexican, you really speak excellent English."

Their identity is further marked by their skin color and religion, inasmuch as the majority are brown and Roman Catholic. In bipolar, segregated U.S. society, where, until some few years ago, "colored" meant "black," the brown person fell outside the system. There were public toilets marked "colored" and "white"; if Mexican-Americans tried to go into the one marked "colored," they were chased out by the blacks; if they tried to go into the one marked "white," they were chased out by the whites. The same thing was true in restaurants and hotels.

Roman Catholicism, as it had been handed down by the Spanish missionaries and blended with the ways of the Mexican Indians, had a profound impact on their cultural identity. Fundamentalists said that their Catholicism was pagan and superstitious; newly arrived French and Irish missionaries said that their Catholicism was savage, superficial, and "lacking faith." Fundamentalist and Jansenistic Catholics imposed their religious convictions on the Mexican-American people. Culturally speaking, it is difficult to say which group did the most harm in the assault on their group identity. Mexican Catholics said that they had "forgotten" the true faith, and U.S. Catholics said they had never had the true faith! Yet they were a deeply religious people.

The Chicano (from the Spanish word for Mexican, *mejicano*) movement made some positive strides in resolving this conundrum, by breaking out of the bipolar model. To the question "Are you Mexican or American?" their answer is "I am a Chicano." This is an important first step.

There were two major thrusts in the early Chicano movement. One was a struggle to identify with the Mexican heritage of its forebears—a heritage that many second-generation Mexican-Americans had tried to submerge (a standard ethnic tactic in "blending-pot" America). This included new pride in their Mexican-American past—for example, taking pride in their new, colloquial, living Mexican-American Spanish, and not thinking of it as "broken-down Spanish." They took a newborn pride in *their* language, music, dances, clothing.

The other major thrust in the early Chicano movement was that of separatism, which came from the frustration of not being understood.

Although the intentions of the Chicano movement certainly represented a step forward, the effectiveness of the movement with Mexican-American communities was something else. Many Chicano leaders adopted language and tactics contrary to the language and tactics of the culture whose values they were trying to rediscover and revitalize. At that point the movement needed to be more self-critical.

However mixed or confused or undefined may be the innermost self-identity of the Mexican-American people, elements of its composition are now coming to light at a more rapid pace than ever before. Poets, artists, and musicians are bringing out, through the language of the arts, many ethnic elements that are still beyond scholarly analysis and synthesis.

Public Image

In terms of public image, the overtones of the predominant U.S. listing of Mexican-American characteristics—brown, Spanish-speaking, racially mixed, Roman Catholic—are heavily negative. All the lasting stereotypes about Mexican-Americans have gone unquestioned by the dominant society and have been imposed on the dominated society. But if you hear again and again that you are inferior, good for nothing, incompetent, lazy, you may eventually begin to believe it yourself.[2]

Psychological studies conducted by R. Díaz-Guerrero have shown that one of the greatest needs of Mexican-Americans is that of heightened self-esteem. In compensation for the low self-image drummed into them by "bossism," racism, poverty, and classism, Mexican-Americans often resort to bragging and boasting—which means seeking a false self-image.[3]

As long as Mexican-Americans look upon their origin in terms of inferiority, they themselves accentuate what the dominant society has been telling them. But if they can go back to their origins and see it in terms of *birth pangs*—something painful but full of potential for future life—they will see it not as a curse but as a blessing. The *acceptance* of *mestizaje* is at the root of reversing the Mexican-American inferiority complex.

The *Mestizo Norte-Americano* who is able to see richness at the heart of what formerly appeared to be the essential poverty of the people now has the beginnings of what it will take to change a negative self-image into a positive self-image. The richness lies in the fact that birth out of the two great traditions allows for the choice of the best in both in the forging of a new existence, a new creation.

Power Struggles: The Logic of Oppression and Liberation

What is the situation of the Mexican-American people in relation to the socio-cultural institutions that make up the skeleton and muscle of the U.S. cultural organism?

By way of background, it should be pointed out that Latin American republics have not generally had stable governments. This has been due to both internal and external factors, which are beyond the scope of the present work.

It must be kept in mind here that Latin American populations cannot be understood correctly as "latin-americanized European" populations. They are *mestizo* populations, new peoples. In terms of cultural growth, moreover, they are now passing from infancy to maturity. This does not mean that they are passing suddenly from being a "primitive" to being a "modern, industrialized" people. They may or may not become "modern." What is meant is that they are reaching the maturity of a new people, responsible for shaping the society that will best suit their identity in guiding their lives.

Mexico's birth as a modern nation dates back only to the 1940s. It was not until the 1960s that it was able to celebrate with pride its birth as a *mestizo* people way back in the 1500s. But by way of comparison, Mexico achieved in some three hundred years what took Europeans more than a millennium.

The *Mestizo Norte-Americano* has come out of this experience of instability. The *mestizo* experience has thus been totally different from the U.S. experience, which, in many ways, was a prolongation, purification, and renewal of the British tradition, which had been in evolution for hundreds of years before the American adventure ever began. In the U. S. there was transplantation but never a new birth. North American social and related functions were fairly well established and fixed between 1776 and the Civil War of the mid-1800s.

U.S. socio-cultural institutions are understood here as the underlying apparatus for the working out of the basic American way of life, enshrining the core group values as perceived by the founders of the nation and as developed and interpreted by successive generations. They interrelate with and reinforce one another in a multiplicity of ways. A close study of American history shows a very close working together of the political, economic, military, educational, and religious institutions of the nation. Though there have been internal tensions and conflicts (the issue of slavery, the labor unionization movement, etc.), the institutional *system* as such has not been seriously questioned by most citizens.

There can be no doubt that North American institutions have generally functioned in the service of in-groups, to the detriment of out-groups. Some out-groups have managed to get into the country and into the system. Others have managed to get into the country but not into the system. Still others have been kept out of both.

Against this background, it should not be surprising that the answers I received (in the questionnaire mentioned in the section above) to the question "How do we situate ourselves within the various institutions of the United States?" were mainly negative. Responders used, over and over again, such terms as "patronized," "silenced," "powerless," "alienated," "ignored," "not wanted," "merely tolerated."

This appears to be one of the most serious areas of frustration, anger, and worry within Mexican-American communities. How to penetrate and participate in these institutions appears to be one of the most pressing problems of the moment.

The only *social* institutions that were mentioned consistently in a positive way were the *family (familia)* and the *neighborhood (barrio, barriada)*. It is there that the Mexican-American people experiences belonging and participation. And there is a strong desire to continue with the group despite the fact that it is still largely rejected by the dominant society. The strong sense of *familia* is probably one of the deep roots of the liberation movement that wants to penetrate the U.S. system without having to sell out its cultural identity.

At the level of institutional belonging, the bipolar model of analysis thus seems to be a useful instrument for analyzing the conflictual situation of the Southwest. The outright "war" between in-groups and out-groups has been softening. Psychologists, sociologists, and educators have been discovering and publicizing fallacies in much of what had been accepted as dogmas in various theories of inferiority. They have shown that "inferiority" has often been another name for "victimization," in one group's quest for domination and exploitation vis-à-vis another group.

Today more and more persons from in-groups and out-groups are joining forces to break down the segregative walls of the overarching system and to help outsiders work their way inside. But of course getting in is not the whole solution. "Getting in" and "staying in" require practical know-how if individuals are to function effectively within the system.[4]

In order to change the overall situation, the Mexican-American people must bring about change within the economic, political, educational, and religious configuration of the region where they live. This raises still more as yet unanswered questions.

Can an ethnic group gain political power without educational expertise and economic strength? Can it receive an adequate education to function effectively within the dominant society without the political and economic power to bring it about? In receiving an education adequate to function effectively within the dominant society, will its members not be assimilated to the dominant society? Is emphasis on external ethnic manifestations (clothing styles, music, food) reasonable compensation for a certain degree of interior assimilation? Can a group have and use economic power without being educated in the ways of the predominant economic system? To what degree can someone participate actively in a system without being assimilated to it?

It is the dominant society that sets the norms and projects the images of success, achievement, acceptability, normalcy, and status. It is the dominant group that sets up the educational process that passes on the traditions and values of the dominant society. To what degree do these norms and images change persons who are outside the system but struggling to get inside it and at the same time maintain a cultural identity different from that of the dominant group?

Some of the inherent tensions and unresolved questions of the struggle for liberation of the group might well be brought out by some quotes from an article in *The Chicano Plan for Mental Health*. They are especially significant because of the personal background and professional preparation of the persons involved in the preparation of this study and also because they are typical of the literature that is emerging on this question:

Chicanos are more apt to be concerned with the problem of maintaining and reinforcing the Chicano culture, opposing assimilation, advocating cultural pluralism, and preserving the intrinsic cultural values of *Chicanismo.*

Mental health problems among Chicanos are more rationally and logically attributable to structural deficiencies in the social system— that is, *lack of access to the opportunity system.*

Nowhere is the denial more obvious than in the *educational system.*

Chicanos, moreover, are falling further behind in their understanding of what it takes to *survive in a complex capitalistic system.*

The varied assortment of clinical terms used to describe mental health problems among Chicanos, such as "mental unbalance" and "dysfunction," are more realistically *manifestations of distrust for a socio-economic and political system that Chicanos see as grossly unfair.*

Lacking full access to the opportunity structure, Chicanos see themselves as pawns in a *racist society* in which *white skin* is a *prerequisite* to social and economic success.[5]

Even in a society where whites normally have better opportunities, a white skin alone is no guarantee of success. A certain expertise is also necessary. To what extent can it be acquired without also acquiring something from the structures erected by the cultural-value mechanisms of the dominant group? To what extent can someone strive to be successful within a "successful" structure without interiorizing, to some extent, the cultural basis of the structure?

It seems that this is what happened, in varying degrees, to other ethnic— especially European—immigrant groups in their struggle to break free of their oppression and gain control of the structures that oppressed them: in the process, they were changed; society remained basically the same. They made it in society, but society remade them. They were refashioned in and by the prevailing mentality of materialism, self-worth measured in terms of wealth, efficiency, competition, and pragmatism.

At the social level the *Mestizo Norte-Americano* people, in its quest to enter U.S. socio-cultural institutions, has also the task of asking some critical questions of U.S. society, to help unveil some of the unquestioned assumptions about "free enterprise," democracy, political pluralism, "progress," the absolute threat of communism, the American Dream of a prosperous middle class with fewer and fewer persons at the extremes of poverty and opulence, the "common good."

Out-groups should also seek to help one another in their common interests. They are all components of the "we" in the *"we* versus *they"* model of social analysis. The "they" does not have to be understood in terms of the bulk of the general population. What if the bulk of the population is itself manipulated by a very small group representing the superpowers of the economic world, in league with the holders of political power—at home and in international powerblocks? The goal is not to reinforce the "we versus they" model of society, but to seek a greater participation in the new "common we" which will struggle together for the benefit of everyone.

Maturity

Emergence of New Cultural Symbols

Just as the family is the basic unit of the social system, so language is the basic unit of the system of thought. It is through language that we think, understand, remember, and communicate. The way that a group represents, interprets, and communicates its understanding of reality is its language.

Every cohesive human group has a language, and the specific language of the group is tied in with its identity and uniqueness.

Tensions of the new, emerging people being born in the Southwest are evidenced in the new language appearing there. They do not speak simply English or Spanish; they speak a Spanish that is a new amalgam of English and Spanish. This new language is a *problem* for language scientists and teachers; it certainly is no problem for those who speak it as their mother tongue. Sometimes it is called bicultural, and its speakers are said to be bilingual. But at a deeper level, it is a new language in its own right, the expression of a new cultural identity. It has received elements of language from both its parents and now is beginning to emerge as a unique synthesis—a newborn language, not simply a yoked projection of its parents' languages.

In my opinion, the key emphasis in bicultural education should not be to try to place a young person within two cultures, but to help everyone within the multicultural context to appreciate the birth of a new culture, a new people. The task should be to see, critically and unemotionally, with insight and respect, what is truly humanizing and dehumanizing in each cultural tradition, and try to shape the new cultural identity by pulling together the best elements of each and reducing the harmful elements of each. It is the traditionally dominant group that will have to have the greater humility to face itself openly and admit that it has much to receive, much to learn, from the groups it has previously considered inferior. There is no question of one group "winning" over the other, but of all groups being willing to die a bit to their own egotism and ethnocentrism for the sake of the new creation.

Contemporary art forms of the Southwest give ample evidence that a new identity is beginning to emerge. The philosophers, ideologues, and theologians must now begin to extract the deeper meaning of the new expressions that are coming to light. Something new is happening, and it needs to be conceptualized, verbalized, and communicated so that the new ideas may take on form and become a power within the life of the group. If the newness is not verbalized, researched by the various intellectual disciplines, and taught by the various media of popular communication at work in society, it will continue to be viewed by those outside the social process as something primitive, or exotic, or "cute"—and the danger is that it could become just that. Serious exploration and communication of the new reality in process is fundamental to the life and survival of the process. This internal process is just beginning now—as is the penetration of the sociocultural institutions of the dominant society—but it is beginning.

The symbolic level of the life of a culture is difficult to penetrate, because symbols are at once so obvious to those for whom they are "natural," and yet so difficult to explain to others. Furthermore there are passing symbols of longstanding that do not even pass away.

Symbols are like the "innate ideas" postulated by some philosophers. They are so deeply embedded in group consciousness that they appear to be the unquestioned principles of action. They are the self-evident starting points of everything else, and the basis of the group's "natural law." The full body of the group's self-knowledge can be understood and interpreted in full only when related to the group's primary symbols. They are both prerational and postcritical: they function before we begin to reason and they have a transcendent meaning even after we have studied them critically.

The questionnaire (mentioned above) that I sent out had questions that referred to group symbolism. The responses confirmed what the team at the Mexican-American Cultural Center (San Antonio, Texas) has been discovering is the general situation of the Mexican-American people throughout the U.S.A.

Group Heroes

The heroes of a group are persons who have embodied in their lives, to an exemplary degree, the ideals of the group. They symbolize one or another important aspect of the values cherished by a culture or subculture. They strengthen group identity and give new members concrete models of action. Their inspirational function is not limited to the past; they function also in efforts to transform the present into a future in which those values will be better realized. They thus play a key role in the formulation and transmission of the core values and ideals of the group.

One question posed in the questionnaire was "Who are the heroes that we (children, teenagers, adults) most spontaneously identify with?" Responses fell into three categories: family members (father, mother, older brother), charismatic leaders (John F. Kennedy, Cesar Chavez, Emiliano Zapata), and movie-television personalities (singers, actors, athletes).

First of all, we identify strongly with family members. Particularly strong is love and attachment to one's mother—and, by extension, to the Virgin

Mother of God, *la Guadalupana.* Inasmuch as the family is the child's first school and the first three years of one's life are the most important in shaping the basic personality of the child, this admiration for family members will be an important factor in the shaping of the fundamental personal and group symbols that the child incorporates.

The second series of heroes (charismatic leaders) could certainly contribute to the continuation of the group symbolic system.

But it is the third series (movie and television personalities) that begins the group's restructuralization process. From a very early age, the child is exposed to countless hours of television. The television "message" will have an impact on the child's developing ideas about "models" of being human, of who are good and bad persons, which types are to be liked or disliked, given approval or disapproval. If the television and movie heroes bring out and exalt qualities that contribute to the greatness of the dominant group in society—norms and values enculturated by the dominant group and projected as *"the* way"—the child begins to absorb them as part of what it means to be "accepted," "heroic," "successful," "human."

And this is where a split—and its pain—begins to form at the base of the child's personality. On the one hand, the child venerates family members, but persons like them do not appear on television or in movies except in a "substandard" role, as corrupt or subservient or silly or stupid. The ideas, language patterns, and mannerisms of media heroes are not what the child experiences in family life. The beginnings of a "split image" of "the ideal person to look up to" take form. Which way will the child go? In all probability, we will not isolate young persons from the entertainment media. What alternative is there to the influence they exert?

There is also the point that Mexican-American children do not in general see *professionals* as their heroes. There could be several reasons for this, one being that most Mexican-American adults appear to them to do routine, nonprofessional work. Few among them become charismatic figures, and when they do (Cesar Chavez can be taken as an example) they often are portrayed by the media in "controversial" settings—that is, they are not universally acclaimed; they are opposed by representatives of the dominant sector of society.

Thus at the hero level—"Who inspires me to be like them?"—there is a split. But it need not be destructive; it can be turned into something constructive. The challenge is to develop popular heroes who embody positive ideals that can be seconded by both cultural traditions. And we need not just one or two such heroes, but many.

The Future

Every human group has its utopic ideas, its dreams, of what it wants to become. Utopic ideas give individuals and groups the motivation to struggle with hardships.

Most immigrants to the United States have come for basically the same reason: to find a better life, freedom, material prosperity. It is true that the U.S. government at times has had to be apologetic for keeping out would-be immigrants from other countries. Yet this is far better than having to apologize for using harsh measures to keep inhabitants *in*. With all its faults, the U.S.A. still conjures up for many throughout the world the kind of life that they dream for.

There was general agreement in the responses to the question (in the questionnaire mentioned above), "What do parents hope for (dream of) for their children?"

Although those who answered included some very politicized and highly ideological persons, most answers were expressed in very simple terms: "less suffering and a better life"; "a happy marriage and a little bit better life"; "good, decent jobs as a result of a good education, and a life more free from prejudice"; "an education, get a better job, get ahead in life . . . have an equal opportunity for work"; "that they can be accepted for what they can offer and share with others."

Mexican-Americans want a better life, want to enter the structures of opportunity. For this they need a North American education, but they also want to retain their cultural and linguistic identity. Is this possible? My hypothesis is that not only is this *possible,* it is *necessary* for the future of the new Americanism I envisage.

Group Celebration

In the light of all that has been said so far, the response to the following question (in my questionnaire) should not be surprising: "In what situations do we feel most alive, most free?" The answers all fitted together: in our fiestas, our family reunions, when we are together as a group. The word most often used was "fiestas." We are most alive and free when we are together, in a celebration, not having to explain to others who we are or why we do the things we do.

The *Mestizo Norte-Americano* is by nature very hospitable and gladly welcomes others, whoever they may be. But group members tire of having to explain to outsiders what they have no need to explain to each other: the historical experience at the basis of their group identity. How to explain a deep personal experience to someone who has never had a similar experience?

It is of interest that none of the answers suggested that Mexican-Americans feel alive or free when they are doing "my thing"; all the answers indicated that "feeling alive and free" is necessarily something pertaining to a *group* experience.

In our fiestas—with our dances, music, food, games, jokes—we celebrate who we are. We celebrate our freedom, because, in spite of the many forces of conquest, oppression, and domination, we have remained a free people with a strong inclination to do "our thing." We may not yet be able to *say* who we are, but there is no doubt in our hearts as to who we are. The scientific definitions have not yet emerged, but we know in our inner being that we are *un pueblo naciendo . . . un pueblo marchando hacia el futuro que ya ha comenzado* ("a nascent people . . . a people marching toward the future that has already begun").

Our fiestas are life because we celebrate the passage from death (the end of old groupings) to life (the birth of new groupings). Our fiestas are not an escape (repression), but a resurrection (sublimation)—a rising above and beyond the rational limits of understanding. Only someone who fully shares in our suffering-unto-life experience can fully share and savor the joy of our fiestas.

The Mexican-American people is not afraid of suffering and death—it has been its lot for centuries—but it is finding a new meaning in this suffering and death: that it is the passage to a new existence. The *raza* is the promise of the future being born today.

Chapter 3

LIVING FAITH: RESISTANCE AND SURVIVAL

The deeply religious character of the Mexican-American people was brought into the orbit of Christianity with the coming of the first Christian missioners in the 1500s. They embedded the tenets of the faith in songs, dramatizations, personal devotions, pictures, ceremonies, and *dichos* ("sayings, proverbs") that were easily learned by the people. Profound theological meaning was transmitted through forms that were readily grasped even by children.

Christianity was not so much superimposed upon as implanted and "naturalized" *in* the Mexican-American way of life. The ensemble of the yearly celebrations of the people is equally the *living Christian creed* of the Mexican-American ecclesial community. It does not so much *recite* the creed in an abstract way as *live* it out, celebrate it, and transmit it in real life and in life-filled celebrations. Our confession of faith is lived out in the language, songs, gestures, dramatizations, and symbols of the people. It is our Christian tradition. It is our creed as received, interiorized, and expressed collectively by our faith community.

The creedal expressions of the people are sociological and theological symbols. They are the ultimate expression of the social level and the starting points of the theological. They encase in a tangible capsule the deepest truths, the mysteries, of Christian revelation. They should be neither ignored nor taken for granted, neither phased out nor idolized.

Symbols of Ultimate Identity and Belonging

Ash Wednesday

To anyone who knows anything about the religious practices of the Mexican-American people, it is obvious that one of the most sacred rites of the year is the reception of ashes on Ash Wednesday. For the masses of the people, it has little to do with the beginning of Lent. Lent as a season of self-sacrifice is not really of special interest to the people: the entire year is a time of suffering and abnegation.

On Ash Wednesday Mexican-Americans renew their cultic communion with mother earth. For them the earth has always been sacred and they retain a fundamental identity with it. The earth supports and regenerates life; it *is* life. Living things—plants, animals, humans—come from the earth and fade back into it when they die. And the earth brings forth new life.

Foreigners may come and take away the earth from them, but they cannot take them away from the earth: the people is the living earth, the living earth is the people. When distant from their land, they dream about it, sing about it. They pray that when they die they will be returned to *their* earth, there to be buried.

Their portion of the world's surface is their fundamental rooting in life, their core identity. Their ancestors came from it and returned to it. It has given them life, nourishment, shelter, clothing, a way of life, physical and psychological characteristics, the elements of their religious expressions. They live in gratitude, love, and communion with mother earth. It is God's great gift to them and the best image they know of his creativity.

Through conquest and exploitation, much of their land has been taken away from them. The sacred land—the primordial sacrament of God's continuing creation and goodness—has been divided into private fiefdoms and commercialized. Fences and political boundaries have been set up to keep them from their own land. For them this is the capital sin of *simony*—trafficking in things divine.

To deprive a people of its own land is like depriving children of their mother. Mexican-Americans sense that the earth belongs to them and they to it—like mother and child. On Ash Wednesday they celebrate their personal and collective communion with their earthly basis of belonging and identity.

The rite of ashes becomes all the more significant in this era when Mexican-Americans are living as captives in their own land. They are called "foreigners" and are treated as illegal intruders by another society that imposed itself on them by violence, power plays, and even religion. In their own land, their ways and their religious expressions are despised and looked down on as backward and primitive.

Their children become embarrassed about their identity because the schools and churches of the invaders tell them that the ways of white, Western civilization are best. Culturally speaking, Anglo-American society is kidnapping the children of the Mexican-Americans, taking them out of their own households, their own *familias,* their own *barrios,* their own land.

The rite of ashes affirms and dares to celebrate the core Mexican-American belongingness and suffering. The ashes are a sign of a suffering and death that will not be useless: even if individual persons are wiped out, the people will continue. The ashes of the present fertilize the seeds of the future.

Ash Wednesday is a day of sorrow *and* joy. The ashes are an exterior manifestation of the innermost attitude of the collective soul of the people: suffering but not despair, acceptance but not fatalism, *aguante* ("endurance") but not passive resignation, joy but not frivolity. And hope beyond immediate expectations.

Posada

One of the most popular ritual celebrations of the Mexican-American people, often organized by the *abuelitos* (the "elders," who are the carriers *par excellence* of tradition), is the *posada* ("hospitality" or "shelter" reenactment). The *posada* is a kind of Christmas novena that combines prayer, songs, and games. It is the reenactment of the journey of Joseph and Mary from Nazareth to Bethlehem.

Before the procession through the *barrio,* there is an opening hymn that sets the theme of the *posada*-novena, reminding the people of the meaning of what is about to take place. One group of persons then walks from house to house carrying statues of Joseph, Mary, and the donkey. Inside each house there is a small group representing the Judeans who reject them one by one, telling them there is no room for them. Finally the small group in one of the houses invites the shelterless couple in and there is great joy in the place that welcomes them.

The apparently artless prayer-ritual text and celebration were in fact very carefully prepared by the early missioners to Mexico, concerned as they were that the essence of the gospel message reach the masses in a simple, comprehensible, and enjoyable way. Behind the gamelike appearances of the celebration, the essence of the gospel message not only came through, but was *retained* and *transmitted* from generation to generation *by the people*. A clergy at a later date, not recognizing the religious content of the *posada*, tried to substitute a cerebral catechesis for its living catechesis.

The introductory prayer-song is as follows. The words in bold type have a special significance, to be explained at the end of the text:

Una bella pastorcita
caminaba por el frío,
y como bella rosita
va cubierta de rocío.

**A beautiful shepherdess
was walking** in the cold,
and, like a beautiful rose,
she was covered with dew.

Caminando va José,
caminando va María.
Caminan para Belén
mas de noche que de día.

Joseph was **walking,**
Mary was **walking.**
They **walked** toward Bethlehem
More by night than by day.

Caminan de tienda en tienda,
no hay lugar en el mesón.
Todos les cierran la puerta
y tambien el corazón.

They **walked** from tent to tent;
there was no room in the inn.
All of them closed their door
and their hearts to them.

Humildes **peregrinos**,
Jesús, María, y José,
mi alma os doy, con ella
mi corazón también.

Humble **pilgrims**,
Jesus, Mary, and Joseph,
I give you my soul, and with it
my heart as well.

La Estrella María

Mary the Star

¿Quién esa estrella
que a los hombres guía?
¡La Reina del Cielo,
la Virgen María!

Who is that star
that guides everyone?
The Queen of Heaven,
the Virgin Mary!

Vamos **caminando**
siguiendo la huella
todos preguntando
quien es esa estrella.

We are **walking**,
following the footprints;
all are asking
who is that star.

Para redimirnos
de la idolatría
vino a este mundo
la Virgen María.

To redeem us
from idolatry
there came to this world
the Virgin Mary.

Las plantas florecen
al ver su grandeza;
los campos se alegran
al ver su belleza.

The plants bloom
at the sight of her greatness;
the fields rejoice
to see her beauty.

Que alegre camino
se ve en esta tierra;
todos de rodillas
estamos con ella.

What a happy road
is seen in this land;
all of us, kneeling,
are with her.

Ya supe quien eres,
madrecita bella,
de amor y placer
reluciente estrella.

I know now who you are,
beautiful mother,
of love and joy,
the shining star.

The emphasized words and phrases embody the theme of "following the way"—the brunt of the Christian gospel preached to the people: *caminando siguiendo la huella,* "we are walking, following the footprints." They are to walk as did the migrant shepherdess from Galilee, walking through the darkness *(mas de noche que de día)* of rejection *(todos les cierran la puerta y tambien el corazón)* toward the light *(estrella)* that will redeem them from the idolatry of the ways of the world *(para redimirnos de la idolatría).*

The house-to-house procession then takes place, the Galilean couple— Joseph and Mary—seeking shelter *(posada)* and the Judean residents refusing their request. The pilgrimage song is as follows; the stanzas sung by those representing Joseph and Mary (in Roman print) are followed by the answers of the Judeans (in italic print):

En nombre del cielo	In the name of heaven
os pido posada	I ask you for lodging,
pues no puede andar	because to keep on going
mi esposa amada.	my beloved wife is unable.

Aquí no es mesón,	*This is not an inn;*
sigan adelante,	*continue on your way;*
y no puedo abrir,	*I can't open [the door];*
no sea algun tunante.	*you may be riffraff.*

No seas inhumano,	Don't be inhuman;
Ténnos caridad,	have charity for us
que el Dios de los cielos	that the God of heaven
te lo premiará.	may repay you for it.

Ya se puedan ir	*You may go now*
y no molestar,	*and don't bother us,*
porque si me enfado	*because if I get angry*
os voy a apalear.	*I'm going to hit you.*

Venimos rendidos	We are very tired,
desde Nazaret.	coming from Nazareth.
Yo soy carpintero	I am a carpenter,
de nombre José.	Joseph by name.

No me importa el nombre,	*I don't care about your name;*
déjenme dormir,	*let me sleep;*
pues que ya les digo	*I already told you*
que no hemos de abrir.	*that we're not going to open.*

After the pilgrim group has been rejected by a number of households, one of them finally takes an interest and agrees to give them a place to stay:

Posada te pide, amado casero, por solo una noche la Reina del Cielo.	Asking you for lodging, kind homeowner, for only one night, is the Queen of Heaven.
Pues si es una reina *quien lo solicita,* *¿como es que noche* *anda tan solita?*	*If she is a queen* *who is asking,* *how is that at night* *she is walking alone?*
Mi esposa es María, es reina del Cielo, y madre va a ser del Divino Verbo.	My wife is Mary, she is the Queen of Heaven, and she is going to be mother of the Divine Word.
¿Eres tú José? *¿Tu esposa es María?* *Entren peregrinos,* *no los conocía.*	*Are you Joseph?* *Your wife is Mary?* *Come in, pilgrims,* *I did not know who you were.*
Dios pague, señores, vuestra caridad y así os colme el cielo de felicidad.	May God reward, good persons, your charity, and may heaven fill you with happiness.
¡Dichosa la casa *que abriga este día* *a la Virgen pura,* *la hermosa María!*	*Happy the home* *that houses today* *the pure Virgin,* *the beautiful Mary!*
Entren santos peregrinos, *reciban este rincón* *no de esta pobre morada* *sino de mi corazón.*	*Come in, holy pilgrims,* *accept this corner,* *not of this poor house,* *but of my heart.*
Esta noche es de alegría, *de gusto y de rogocijo,* *porque hospedamos aquí* *a la Madre de Dios Hijo.*	*This is a night of happiness,* *of joy and rejoicing,* *because we give hospitality here* *to the Mother of God the Son.*

The rite is centered on two experiences that bring out key themes of the gospel proclamation: the *rejection* of the poor, nameless couple from the "inferior" region of Galilee, and the *joy* that comes to those who open the door of their home and heart to shelter and welcome the rejects, because they recognize them for what they truly are: God's chosen ones. It is in the poor shepherd girl from Nazareth that God now dwells. Her womb is the new temple of God's presence. God comes to make his abode among us in those whom the world rejects.

These central experiences are to be repeated in the life of Jesus. He comes from a multiply rejected people. He experiences both the pain of rejection by those who judge themselves "superior," and the joy of being accepted and welcomed by his own.

Whereas wealthy Mexicans have turned the *posada* into an elaborate and expensive drunken brawl that has nothing to do with its original meaning, the poor and simple continue the tradition of the original *posada*. And they enter into the beginnings of the way of Jesus. Whether the church encourages them or not, these living Christian catechetical novenas continue in all *barrios* where Mexicans or Mexican-Americans live. The *posada* has taken place for hundreds of years, passed on from generation to generation, without written rituals or scripts.

The *posada* is easily a *cultic* reminder and reenactment as well, for Mexican-Americans who have walked, often at night and through snake-infested deserts, to the U.S.A. in the hope of finding work. What they found instead was rejection after rejection. But, like Joseph and Mary, they did not give up; they followed their star.

The *posada* is a living symbol of a living faith.

Pastorela

Another popular devotion expressing the theme of human rejection and divine election is that of the *pastorela*. The *pastorelas* are miracle plays that were started by the early missioners to allow the Indians to experience the entire drama of salvation. They started with creation, went through the fall, continued through the various struggles of the chosen people, finally coming to the birth of Christ and the adoration. They were very graphic and visual and included battles between angels and devils, the struggles of the prophets, the temptations by the devils, and finally the great conquest of the coming of Christ. These miracle plays have been handed on from generation to generation, and the scripts have never been written until very recent times. People took it upon themselves as a vow to re-enact their part once a year and to prepare someone who would be able to continue when they were no longer around. *Pastorelas* were put on in the neighborhoods throughout Mexico and in many places of the southwest.

One of the things that always impressed me about the *pastorelas* was that the costumes appeared to be very shabby. I was always tempted to give the people some money so that they could buy finer materials for the costumes. Eventually, I learned from them that there was a profound reason for these types of costumes. Costumes may be made only from discarded materials:

in the incarnation the rejected of the world are chosen and beautified.
Hence the *pastorelas* are themselves a celebration of the rejection that becomes election in the birth of Christ.

St. Martin de Porres

Historians are agreed that the Peruvian Martin de Porres was held back
for a time from full membership in the Dominican Order because of the
church law barring the children of unmarried parents from entering a religious congregation. Or it may have been Martin himself, in his rugged
humility, who would not ask anything for himself except the lowest place.
But the masses of Latin America commonly believe that he was acted
against prejudicially because of his racially mixed parentage (his father was
Spanish, his mother a freed African). God worked extraordinary wonders
through him; he was finally canonized by Pope John XXIII. *San Martín de
Porres* is another example of the lesson that God chooses what humankind
rejects. Church law did not allow him to be called to orders, but God called
him into the communion of saints.

Diosito, Jesús, María y los Santos

Personal intimacy with God is another constant in the Mexican-American
faith. It takes expression in a variety of ways. Many of the ordinary sayings
of daily life are a sign of it: *Si Dios quiere* ("If God wills"); *Hágase la vo-
luntad de Dios* ("God's will be done"); *Que Diosito te ayude* ("May God
help you"); *Adios* (in the meaning: "Leave it to God"); *El hombre pone y
Dios dispone* ("Man proposes, God disposes").

The terms *Diosito* and *Papacito Dios* occur frequently in ordinary con-
versation (from *Dios,* "God," and *Papá,* "father, dad," plus the suffix *-ito,*
a diminutive implying familiarity; there are no direct equivalents in English,
the closest approximations being something like "Dear Little God" and
"Daddy-God").

Reference to God the Father is common in poetry and song. The pa-
ternal, loving, and caring presence of God is an unquestioned fact of everyday life. God is always present to his people; they live in his presence.

In most Mexican-American homes—as in most Mexican homes—a home
altar is to be found, with a crucifix, a picture or statue of Mary (usually Our
Lady of Guadalupe, but sometimes another *"virgencita"* or several different ones together), and a picture of the Sacred Heart. There may be other
statues and pictures, including one of John F. Kennedy or even the local
priest. But the crucifix, the *virgencita,* and the Sacred Heart will almost
always be there in a position of honor. Image-presence has always played a
key role in the life and communication process of the Mexican-American
people.

Westminster United Presbyterian Church
1501 WEST CLEVELAND R...
SOUTH BEND, INDIANA 46628

The Sacred Heart

It is important to know that deep in the Mexican personality *rostro y corazón* ("countenance and heart") have always been the revelation of the human personality in action. The word "heart" continues to be used in Mexican and Mexican-American Spanish to refer to *persons* loved. The heart is the symbol of the person. And because their knowledge or awareness of Christ is not so much through the medium of messianic titles or of doctrine, but through their personal and intimate friendship with Jesus of Nazareth, it is the heart that best expresses it.

The Sacred Heart is the symbol that best images the full reality of Jesus to the Mexican-American: unlimited, unconditioned love. They want to relate to a living Christ who has an understanding face and a compassionate heart. Mexican-Americans are not satisfied with *reading* the truth; they want to *see* the truth. And it is in the image of the Sacred Heart that they "see" the truth of Jesus and the Father fully revealed.

Eucharistic Presence

The presence of Christ in the Eucharist—Corpus Christi processions, the night watch on Holy Thursday, the presence in the tabernacle—has been another sensible and communitarian experience of the closeness of the Lord to the Mexican-American people. The Cursillo movement was especially successful in promoting a keen sense of the real presence of Christ as Lord and brother. I have often observed Mexican-Americans kneeling before the Blessed Sacrament, discussing their problems and hopes—and I find it very natural to do so myself.

Christ the King

As the masses of the Mexican people became more and more dissatisfied with the abuses heaped on them by successive governments, they became convinced that Christ alone could be trusted as ruler and king. In contrast to the European experience, where devotion to Christ the King seems to have been promoted as a final defense of monarchy, in Mexico it became the symbol of ultimate defiance to a tyrannical government. If politicians could not be trusted, then in the name of the true king, Christ the Lord, they must be overthrown.

In the late 1920s the Cristero movement (from *Cristo Rey*) reproached the Mexican government for its ban on all religious services in the nation's Catholic churches and other restrictive measures. The solemnities of Christ the King were celebrated throughout the nation despite the government's stand. In Mexico City two hundred thousand persons paraded through the streets shouting *"¡Viva Cristo Rey, Viva la Virgen Morena, Viva el Papa,*

Viva el arzobispo, Viva el clero mexicano!" ("Long live Christ the King . . . the Dark Virgin . . . the pope . . . the archbishop . . . the Mexican clergy!").

Inasmuch as the Mexican and Mexican-American peoples have never lived under a government that was truly for the people and by the people, the theme of the kingdom of *Cristo nuestro Rey* continues to be very real in their lives. It is not something separate from the theme of rejection and acceptance, but a development and implementation of it. In the theme of the kingdom some of the nuclear aspects of the way of Jesus are brought out more explicitly: intimacy with the Father is blended with intimacy with Jesus, with the saints, with one another. The fundamental equality and dignity of each person is affirmed as the only true basis of human society and governance.

Symbols of Struggle, Suffering, and Death

It should not be surprising that devotion to the crucified Lord— scourged, bleeding, agonizing—is one of the deepest traits of the Mexican-American faith. *Cruz* ("cross") is a not uncommon name given to their children.

El Viernes Santo (Good Friday) is the Mexican-American celebration *par excellence*. The commemoration of the Lord's crucifixion is the celebration of their life—a life of suffering. Their daily life is assumed in his death and therein defies the anomalies of life.

Why is the "scandal" of the cross as necessary for salvation today as it was for Jesus? Because the cross continues to reveal the impurity of the pure and the purity of the impure, the innocence of criminals and the crimes of the innocent, the righteousness of sinners and the sin of the righteous, the wisdom of the foolish and the foolishness of the wise.

Some persons working with Mexican-Americans have thought it would be better to shift the emphasis from the cross to the resurrection. I would agree *if* the situation were changing in such a way that we could say that resurrection was indeed becoming a meaningful symbol. But this is not yet the case. I agree with Jesuit theologian Jon Sobrino that the point is not to do away with the people's celebration of the cross, but to help them appreciate better Jesus' active march toward the cross, and not just the passive aspect of suffering on the cross. In the long run, of course, this march would be meaningless without the resurrection; human suffering, as imaged in the crucifixion, would be devoid of sense. Jesus did not *start* with the cross, nor was it the only element in his salvific ministry.

The drama of Good Friday is not just celebrated ritually in the churches but lived out by the Mexican-American people. Beginning on Holy Thursday with the agony in the garden, on Good Friday the way of the cross is reenacted by the people, then the crucifixion, and the seven last words of Jesus from the cross. Finally, in the evening, there is the *pésame a la Virgen* ("visit to the Virgin"). Never was the distance between the "official" church and the church of the people more evident to me than on Good Friday in Mexico City where there might be as few as 100 persons in a *barrio* church for the official services, and as many as 60,000 outside the church, taking part in a living way of the cross.

To "academic" theologians and liturgists this may seem a folkloric, nostalgic, emotional, childish expression of religion; they would not call it *real* liturgy. But for a people for whom sudden arrest, speedy trial, trumped-up charges, circumstantial evidence, quick verdict, and immediate sentencing are a way of life—as is true for the millions of poor and oppressed throughout Latin America and in the U.S.A.—this ritual reenactment of the way of Jesus is the *supreme* liturgy. It is the celebration of their creed. It is not academic theorization; it is life.

Mary's role in the crucifixion of her Son is relived by millions of women in Latin America—grandmothers, mothers, wives, girlfriends. They stand by silently as injustice, violence, is done to their loved ones. They are silent not because they are afraid or because they agree with the civil authorities, but because they do not even understand the language. They are silent because they know, through their collective experience with other women who have gone through similar experiences, that they are powerless against the authorities: *"Pues no sé, Padrecito, se lo llevaron las autoridades . . . no hay nada que se pueda hacer"* ("I don't know, the authorities took him away, Padre . . . there's nothing to be done"). They are silent not only because they do not have the money to hire a lawyer, but because they probably do not even know about the existence of lawyers. They are silent because if they said something reprisals might be taken against other members of the family.

Thousands of persons watch their loved ones be taken away, accused of some crime, condemned, and sentenced by the "justice of the powerful"—and all they can do is stand silently by them to the very end. I have myself met many such men and women in the jails of San Antonio. They do not even know why they are there. Some just happened to be standing by when a crime was committed. Their family has no money for bail. They do not know their way around. All they could do was pray and patiently wait and hope that something would be worked out.

The final Good Friday reenactment is the burial service. Some ridicule this popular rite of the burial of Jesus and attribute its popularity to the "morbid" inclinations of the Mexican-Americans—"always preoccupied with death." But when it is realized that even in death this people is rejected, the quiet, almost clandestine, burial of Jesus takes on a deeper significance for them. Segregated cemeteries are still a commonplace, even if not segregated as in the past—along skin-color lines.

The Mexican-American people has a very special devotion to *nuestro Diosito en la cruz.* Good Friday is *nuestra fiesta,* the cultic celebration of *nuestra existencia.* It is not an "other-worldly" make believe; it is a celebration of *nuestra vida.*

Symbols of New Creation

The happiness and joy of the Mexican and Mexican-American peoples is immediately obvious to outsiders. The tragedies of their history have not obliterated laughter and joy, warm friendship and the capacity to love.

The Mexican-American propensity for celebration is something that others find extremely difficult to understand. Outsiders may enjoy but they cannot enter fully into the spirit of a fiesta or imitate one on their own. But anyone who has attended a Mexican-American fiesta knows that celebration has taken place. There is spontaneity and ritual, joy and sorrow, music and silence.

Fiesta is the mystical celebration of a complex identity, the mystical affirmation that life is a gift and is worth living. In the fiesta the fatalistic/pessimistic realism and the adventuresome/optimistic idealism of the Mexican heritage are blended into the one celebration of the mystery of life—a series of apparent contradictions never fully comprehended but assumed, transcended, celebrated. In the fiesta the Mexican-American rises above the quest for the logical meaning of life and celebrates the very contradictions that are of the essence of the mystery of human life.

The Fiesta of Our Lady of Guadalupe

Two Mexican-American celebrations stand out as the most universal: the collective celebration of the fiesta of Our Lady of Guadalupe and the family celebration of the baptism of an infant. The two celebrations are interrelated in the identification of the people as *la raza* as a cultural and religious entity.

Because of the historical process that has been taking place over the past four hundred years and continues today, the cultural elements in the Mexican-American identity cannot be fully separated from the religious elements. The gospel and the culture are not fully identified with each other, but they cannot be fully separated. The gospel has been transforming the culture and the culture has been reactualizing the gospel through its own vital expressions.

If Ash Wednesday stresses the earthly belonging and present suffering of the people, and Good Friday marks their collective struggles and death, the feast of Our Lady of Guadalupe shouts out with joy the proclamation that a new dawn is breaking: the collective resurrection of a new people. Out of their own earth—Tepeyac—and in continuity with the life of their ancestors, a new mother emerges, pregnant with new life. She is not a goddess but the new woman from whom the new humanity will be born, *la raza cósmica de las Américas*. She is herself the prototype of the new creation. She is *la Mestiza*. She combines opposing forces so that in a creative way new life, not destruction, will emerge. On December 12 is celebrated the beginning of the new human-divine adventure.

It is important to remember that *flowers* were the sign that *la Morenita* gave to prove that she was God's messenger. In ancient and contemporary Mexican culture, flowers are a sign of new existence. From the seeds that fall to earth, are watered by the heavenly dew, and fertilized by the ashes and remains of previous life, new life comes forth.

The resurrection of Christ was the beginning of the new Christian people, uniting and transcending natural peoples without destroying them. Something similar happened at Guadalupe. Mexicans discovered that they were a new people, reborn.

On the feast of Our Lady of Guadalupe, the people come together early in the morning to celebrate the irruption of new life—the dawn of a new humanity. This is the Easter sunrise service of the people. Before the first rays of the sun, they come together to sing *Las Mañanitas* which is our proclamation of new life. It is the roses of Tepeyac that take the place of the Easter lillies of western Christianity.

Guadalupe was also a *pentecost* event: it opened the way to true dialogue between Europeans and Mexican Indians. It was a symbol of unity over and above their many and serious diversities. It marked the beginning of the fusion of two mother cultures—the Spanish and the Mexican Indian— which in turn gave birth to a *mestizo* culture. *La Morenita* became the "mother of all the inhabitants of this land." Individuals who found themselves divided and segregated on the basis of human barriers—external differences—discovered that they were united in something far more important than what divided them: a common mother. Mexico is a very divided nation, and there is no doubt to anyone working with Mexican-Americans in the U.S.A. that they constitute a very divided people. But there is likewise a very strong unity and spirit of *familia* among this divided people.

It has been held that the symbolism of Guadalupe works to canonize and maintain *divisions* among the Mexican-American people. I have to admit that in some ways this does happen. But there is another function to the symbol: it gives a basis for a much deeper unity than does any class-struggle model. The power of Guadalupe is that it signals a common motherhood for all the inhabitants of the land. As new models of society are proposed and begin to be worked out, as long as they lead to or allow some individuals to think of themselves as inferior and others as superior, the conviction of a fellowship of equals under a common mother cannot find realization. Conversely, when individuals have become aware of their basic equality and see that it is not embodied in their society, they will work and struggle to bring about new lifestyles more reflective of the fundamental reality that all are children of the same mother.

La Morenita is found not only in the basilica in Mexico City but in numberless shrines throughout the Americas, in the homes of millions of persons, on medals around the necks of men, women, and children, tattooed on the arms and chests of men, sung about in pop songs, painted on the walls of *barrios* from California to Texas. Our Lady did not appear once and for all in 1531: she continues to appear wherever Mexican-Americans find themselves in the world today.

Our Lady did not simply tell the Indians to build her a temple. She sent them to the bishop—the representative of the institutional church. It was to be the *people*—the whole church—that would build the new temple of compassion. The message was twofold: the Indians, in the person of Juan Diego, were to go to the bishop (the church), and the church (in the person of the bishop) was to build a temple among the people.

In her telling the people through Juan Diego "Go to the bishop . . . ," we can glimpse a reflection of her telling the waiters at Cana "Do whatever he tells you . . ." (John 2:5). And what she tells the church is to "build a temple . . . of compassion"—a way of life in which compassion, mercy, love will reign. In other words, her command, understood in this broader sense, was: "Incarnate the gospel among this people, so that Christ will not come as a stranger but as one of them."

Mary's command to the Mexican church in 1531 was echoed by the Synod of Bishops in 1977, when it recognized and stressed the obligation on the part of the church to inculturate the gospel among the peoples of diverse cultures, in order for it to be understood and lived by them. Without this inculturation—*mestizaje*—of the gospel into the natural substratum of a people's life, the gospel will never truly be implanted and a truly local church will never emerge.

Baptism

In the seven years that followed the apparition at Guadalupe in 1531, some eight million persons came to the church asking for baptism. They came in large groups and from great distances, reminiscent of the baptisms following the sermons of St. Peter in the infant church.

Baptism has always played a very special role in the lives of the Mexican and Mexican-American peoples. The baptized infant enters into the collective identity and life of the family, the group, and the people. Baptism has never been thought of as simply the entry of another individual into the institutional church. In baptism the child is accepted and welcomed (recall the *posada* imagery) into the life and memory of the entire family—parents, siblings, grandparents, relatives, and in-laws. The newly baptized becomes *uno de los nuestros* ("one of ours"). What the people celebrate collectively on the feast of Guadalupe, they celebrate individually in the baptism of a child: rebirth and the promise of new life.

That the gospel has penetrated and permeated the Mexican-American culture is beyond question. We turn now to a rereading of that normative gospel experience—matrix—so that from it, one might discover the ultimate meaning of the Mexican-American situation and the direction its struggle must take.

PART TWO

The Gospel Matrix

As deep as the christianization of the Mexican-American people and its culture has been, the task is far from complete. Our people, like all Christian peoples, still must be judged by the word of the gospel.

We must be aware that we, like all Christians, are historico-culturally conditioned and that we read the gospels from within our conditioned perspective. This is both our limitation and our originality. We need to do a serious rereading of the gospels to discover how Jesus of Nazareth functioned in relation to *his* history and culture. By discovering how he functioned *then,* we will discover how he functions *today.* This type of rereading will turn up previously hidden aspects of the gospel message. This type of culturally conditioned rereading of the gospels will contribute to the universal church's growth in understanding the full impact of the liberating mystery of Christ.

Keeping the present-day faith community in mind, the ministry of theology turns to the *normative* experience of the faith community—the tradition of the church, especially the founding tradition of the Christian church as recorded in the New Testament and the writings of the church fathers of the earliest centuries. The insights—the "plan"—gained by this reading of the aboriginal tradition must then be compared with the picture we have of the local, contemporary church, to look for areas of convergence and divergence, seeing our way through to allowing the way of Jesus to come alive in the faith community today. Without this corrective reinterpretation we can easily confuse the cultural expression of *our* faith with *the* faith, and begin to impose our cultural expressions of the gospel on *the* gospel. By the same token, if the gospel is not reinterpreted through the expressions, language, and symbols of the faith community, it will appear as a foreign, lifeless, or even destructive doctrine, not an incarnated, life-giving power.

This undertaking is not, as such, a work of biblical exegesis or of dogmatic or moral theology, but of *pastoral theology:* the pastor, as the teacher and animator of God's revealed truth, seeks to channel the word of

47

God, its meaning and power, to a specific faith community today. We take the exegetical studies of biblical experts seriously, but we do not attempt to simply reproduce or broadcast them; we want to bring out their concrete, salvific implications. What specific *changes* does the word of God bring about in persons and society? What real differences does it make? It is the task of the pastoral theologian to bring out the human meaning of the divine message and the divine meaning of the human situation.

Chapter 4

THE GALILEE EXPERIENCE

Jesus came from Nazareth
of Galilee [Mark 1:10].

The overwhelming originality of Christianity is the basic belief of our faith that not only did the Son of God become a *human being,* but he became *Jesus of Nazareth.* Like every other man and woman, he was culturally situated and conditioned by the time and space in which he lived. The God of Jesus cannot be known unless Jesus is known (John 12:44–45, 14:9). And we cannot really know Jesus of Nazareth unless we know him in the context of the historical and cultural situation of his people. Jesus was not simply a Jew, he was a Galilean Jew; throughout his life he and his disciples were identified as Galileans.

Galilee must have had a special significance to the postresurrection Christian community: it is mentioned sixty-one times in the New Testament, yet hardly appears in the Old Testament. Older Jewish sources do not seem to relate the coming of the Messiah with Galilee; it was only some late rabbinical and cabalistic texts that view Galilee as the site of Messianic events.[1]

The greatest part of the public ministry of Jesus and many of the incidents that are best known to ordinary Christians took place in Galilee, or near it, or on the road between Galilee and Jerusalem. Some of those events were: Jesus' first summons to conversion; the first proclamation of the kingdom of God; the wedding feast at Cana; his first preaching, in the synagogue at Nazareth; his visit to Mary and Martha; the first calling of disciples; many cures; the miraculous catch of fish; the pardon and healing of the paralytic; the Sermon on the Mount; the Lord's Prayer; the golden rule; the cure of the centurion's daughter; the following of Jesus on his way; the calming of the sea; the parables of the good Samaritan, the lost sheep, the prodigal son, and others; the feeding of the multitude; the walking on the water; Peter's confession; Jesus' announcement of his decision to set out for Jerusalem.

His apostles were Galileans and it was in Galilee that they were called to follow him (Matt. 10:1–4; Mark 3:13–19; Luke 10:1–4). Peter, the spokesman of the group, was easily recognized as a Galilean by other Jews during the trial of Jesus (Matt. 26:69–75; Mark 14:66–72; Luke 22:56–62). Peter could deny Jesus, but he could not deny he was a Galilean. After Pentecost, the disciples were recognized as Galileans by the crowds in Jerusalem (Acts 2:7).

It was from Galilee that the resurrected Lord sent them forth to make disciples of all nations (Matt. 28:16–20; John 21:1–25).

Nonetheless, it seems that the theological significance of Galilee was not taken as a point of interest for students of the New Testament in later centuries. From the beginning of the present century, it was understood better as the place of the eschatological fulfillment of the hopes of Judaism, but it is only within the last thirty years that the theological prominence of Galilee has reappeared. Its nonimportance to scholars, until recent times, is evidenced by the fact that the famous *Theological Dictionary of the New Testament* by Kittel does not even have an article on Galilee.

In the past, theological interpretations of Galilee were generally restricted to particular passages, such as Mark 14:28 and 16:7. Within recent times, E. Lohmeyer,[2] R. H. Lightfoot,[3] and W. Marxsen[4] have pointed to Galilee as a major theological motif influencing the entire gospel of Mark and, to a lesser degree, that of Matthew and John.

In a very interesting and revealing article on the theological symbolism of Galilee in John's gospel, Wayne Meeks writes: "The puzzling question which still remains is: how precisely did Galilee and Samaria become positive symbols for the Christian movement?" And he notes: "There is no hint that they were derived from scripture proofs."[5] He notes too that there are many assumptions about this, but no final conclusion.

As more and more scholars get into the area of the theological meaning of Galilee, there are increasingly divergent views as to its exact meaning. Our purpose is not to repeat what scholars have been saying on the theme of Galilee at the redactional level of the gospels, but rather to ask other questions: what is the meaning of Galilee at the level of the historical Jesus who certainly originated from Nazareth in Galilee, and who made his historic journey from there to Jerusalem? If it is not important to the Old Testament yet appears to be a key symbol in the New Testament and even an integral pattern of the primitive kerygma, then possibly its theological significance is to be found outside the Old Testament.

The New Testament uses "Galilee" and "Galilean" in diverse ways. Conscious of the various symbolic interpretations given to Galilee by different scholars, I maintain that all these meanings are rooted in the fact that Jesus grew up and began his work there. The symbolic richness of Galilee must be sought in its historico-cultural identity: a crossroads of cultures and peoples with an openness to each other.

Galilee: Symbol of Multiple Rejection

If it had not been for Jesus of Nazareth, Galilee would have continued to be just another unknown region of the world. A beautiful region, it was especially fertile around the area of the Lake of Galilee. For those who knew of it, it might have appeared primitive and exotic.[6] A convenient crossroads, Galilee was neither a religious nor an intellectual center; it did not wield political power. According to biblical literature it appears to have been outside the mainstream of Israelite life. When Galilee fell to the Assyrians after the Syro-Ephraimite War of 735 B.C., some of its inhabitants were the first to be sent into exile. They were reassured, however, that in the end God would restore the ravaged lands to their former glory. In one of the most important messianic passages of the Old Testament, the prophet Isaiah acknowledges the misery of their life, but out of a vision of ruin a promise of restoration is given to them. The restoration will come through "a child [who] will be given to us" (Isa. 9:5).

The history of the region witnessed multiple invasions by various groups and its geographical setting made it a natural crossing place for international travel routes. Its people were in continual contact with world trade and culture; the region became very cosmopolitan.

Its population was very heterogeneous and became more so after the downfall of the Ephraimite kingdom. From 734 B.C. onward, the region passed through Assyrian, Babylonian, Persian, Macedonian, Egyptian, and Syrian rule, infiltration, and migration. Such was the setting when Jesus came into that world. If for no other reason than commerce, the Jews were friendly and accommodating to non-Jews. The Roman policy favored development of commerce as a means of increasing taxes and also as a way of "cooling" the revolutionary Galileans: a happy, prospering people would be less prone to foment a revolution.

At the time of Jesus, Galilee was peopled by Phoenicians, Syrians, Arabs, Greeks, Orientals, and Jews. In this mixed, commerce-oriented society, some Jews had allowed their Jewish exclusivism to weaken, but others became more militantly exclusivist. Some of the *goyim* (non-Jews) converted to Judaism and intermarried with Jews. Some religious ideas of other groups were also assimilated, as is evident in the case of the Essenes.[7] A natural, ongoing biological and cultural *mestizaje* was taking place.

The Jews were scorned by the Gentiles, and the Galilean Jews were regarded with patronizing contempt by the "pure-minded" Jews of Jerusalem. The natural *mestizaje* of Galilee was a sign of impurity and a cause for rejection. The Pharisees looked down upon "the people of the land" because they were ignorant of the law. The Sadducees looked down upon them because they were somewhat lax in matters of religious attendance and familiarity with the rules of temple worship. The New Testament (John 7:52) gives further evidence of the widespread negative image of Galilee.

Yet throughout all this the Galileans maintained a refreshing originality in Judaism. It was a combination of the commonsense, grass-roots wisdom of practical expertise, their more open and personal relations with foreigners, and their relative distance from Jerusalem. Their hospitable and fertile land gave them a warmer, more optimistic outlook on life than the Judean Jews had. Distance from Jerusalem and daily contact with foreigners were characteristic of the Galilean Jew. The intellectual preoccupation of Jerusalem, with its various schools, hardly reached Galilee. The Galilean faith in the God of the fathers was thus more personal, purer, simpler, and more spontaneous. It was not encumbered or suffocated by the religious scrupulosities of the Jewish intelligentsia.

Although the Pharisees had penetrated into Galilee, there appears to have been no famous school of the group in the region. The Galilean Pharisees with their synagogues were not a large group. It would seem that the relation of the ordinary people to the intellectual Pharisees was much the same as the relation of the ordinary person to the intellectual of today. The rigorous religious intellectuals castigated the Galileans for allowing their religion to be contaminated with foreign ways, for being lax, ignorant of the law, and therefore incapable of pure Jewish piety. Because they were not able to pronounce certain sounds, they were mocked and laughed at by educated persons, both Greek and Jewish. The slurring of the guttural sounds especially aroused contempt. The rabbis considered that this defective pronunciation precluded the Galileans from studying the law. Galileans were sometimes forbidden to recite the public prayers in the synagogue.

The image of the Galileans to the Jerusalem Jews is comparable to the image of the Mexican-Americans to the Mexicans of Mexico. On the other hand, the image of the Galileans to the Greco-Romans is comparable to the image of the Mexican-American to the Anglo population of the United States. They were part of and despised by both.

There was, however, one strong, unifying symbol that obtained for all Jews: the God of Moses and of the prophets. In spite of the many differences and images of one other, they were conscious of a deeper unity: they were all children of the God who revealed himself in and through their history; they all believed in the God who would redeem and save his people. How each one interpreted this did differ, but the fundamental symbol that was the basis of their existence was the same for all.

Between the Diaspora Jews and the Galilean Jews there was a parallelism of perspective in relation to the law. Since the days of Antiochus IV Epiphanes, the Diaspora Jews began to distinguish between God's law and human laws. They stressed God's creation as the foundation of all laws— ethical and socio-ethical—and purity as an internal disposition of the heart rather than a matter of externals.

Galilee was the home of the simple people—that is, of the people of the land, a hardworking people, marginated and oppressed regardless of who was in power or what system of power was in effect. They were the ones who were left out and exploited by everyone else. They shared the fate of other peoples living on the margins of "better" civilizations. Nobody looks for leadership from or has high expectations of those who live in the sticks, the *barrios,* the *ranchitos,* or inner-city slums.

In the light of the entire message of the New Testament, the systematic identification of Jesus with the poor and rejected of society might give us the necessary clue to the importance, signification, and function of Galilee. Scripturally speaking, Galilee does not appear important in the unfolding drama of salvation and, culturally speaking, at the time of Jesus, it was rejected and despised by the Judean Jews because of the racial mixture of the area and its distance from the temple in Jerusalem. For the Jews of Jerusalem, Galilean was almost synonymous with fool!

The apparent nonimportance and rejection of Galilee are the very bases for its all-important role in the historic eruption of God's saving plan for humanity. The human scandal of God's way does not begin with the cross, but with the historico-cultural incarnation of his Son in Galilee. The Galilean Jews appear to have been despised by all and, because of the mixture of cultures of the area, they were especially despised by the superiority-complexed Jerusalem Jews. Could anything good come out of such an impure, mixed-up, and rebellious area? Yet it is precisely within this area of multiple rejection that the restlessness for liberation and the anxiety for the kingdom of God was the greatest.

Without referring to the Galilean theme as such, St. Paul's fundamental idea of the election of the world's nobodies expresses the same core idea as brought out by Mark with the term "Galilee." It can be said that the geographical theme "Galilee" in the gospels is the same as the theme of the election of "what is nothing" *(ta mē onta)* in the Pauline writings. God has demonstrated the wisdom of this world to be foolishness and has called not the intellectual, the powerful, not the important of society, but the insignificant, the weak, and the despised (1 Cor. 1:18–31). "He calls into being what is not" (Rom. 4:12). To be a Galilean Jew was already to be one of the ignorant, insignificant, and despised of the world. That God had chosen to become a Galilean underscores the great paradox of the incarnation, in which God becomes the despised and lowly of the world. In becoming a Galilean, God becomes the fool of the world for the sake of the world's salvation.

What the world rejects, God chooses as his very own. This theme of worldly rejection-divine election is substantiated in the earliest preaching of the Church when Peter proclaimed: "This Jesus is 'the stone rejected by you builders which has become the cornerstone' " (Acts 4:11).

In the wisdom of God, it is precisely here in this impure, culturally mixed, freedom-loving, rebellious region that God made the historical beginning of his visible reign on earth. One cannot follow the way of the Lord without appreciating the scandalous way of Jesus the Galilean.

The Kingdom of the Father:
Symbol of Universal Acceptance, Welcome, and Love

The brunt of the Galilean ministry can be summed up in one phrase: "All of you, especially those who have been rejected, are invited to come into the kingdom of my Father." The immediate consequence: conflicts with those

who had maintained exclusive privileges of status, respectability, and belonging.

The core, dynamic symbol of the Jewish people will become the central
symbol of the message of Jesus, but Jesus will unveil aspects of it unsuspected by the people and unwanted by many of them. In revealing new aspects of the kingdom, Jesus will reveal not only new insights into the understanding of God, but likewise new insights into the understanding of the
human person.

To appreciate the meaning of the kingdom of God as lived and proclaimed by Jesus, it is important to note three key themes that have an important function and around which other ideas may be grouped: (a) the
geographico-symbolic meaning of the Galilean identity; (b) the intimacy of
Jesus with God the Father and his intimacy with all persons, especially the
most rejected, inviting them all into a common intimacy with God the
Father; (c) the transition from the Galilean ministry to the Jerusalem ministry. In using the symbol of the kingdom of God, Jesus not only reaffirms
the constant belief of Israel—that it was God's people and that God was
active in history in its behalf—but he also widens and expands the meaning
of the symbol beyond all imagined expectations.

Jesus the Galilean: A Borderland Reject

Every human society—political, ethnic, religious . . . or whatever it may
be—appears to develop ways of accepting and welcoming some persons
while rejecting and downgrading others. Every society develops its own
ways of determining not only in-groups and out-groups, but even degrees of
being considered "in," and degrees of being considered "out"; the normal
and the abnormal; the successful and the failures; the saints and the sinners;
the city slickers and the country hicks. These categories, in one way or
another, appear to exist within every human grouping.

One such category is geographical place. Where do you come from? The
ordinary stereotypes assign "acceptability" to some places and not to
others. Some are considered all right; others are considered backward and
uncivilized. This becomes evident too when you travel. The passport you
carry will determine where you are welcome, where you will be tolerated,
and where you will not be allowed in. Your place of origin already marks
you as acceptable or unacceptable. Geography marks the ordinary person
who is born and raised in a particular region, for there will be certain mannerisms, gestures, speech- and thought-patterns, and an accent that will
probably identify the individual for life.

From the time of Solomon the land of Galilee had come to be known as
the land of Cabul, which in itself meant "like nothing" or "very displeas-
ing." The connotation remained and the inhabitants of the region came to
be looked down on and considered good for nothing.

Very little is known about the private life of Jesus, but there is no doubt that during his lifetime he was identified as a Galilean. It can be presumed that, like any Jew, he learned the traditions of their national heroes. As he grew up he learned the Shema, the Decalogue, and other passages of the Torah by heart. The law was the essence of the teaching of the synagogue. As in most small, rural communities, the basics were sufficient: children had the example of a religious family upbringing.

Like all Jewish boys it is certain that at home Jesus copied some of the Scriptures. Yet in Galilee it is unlikely that he came into much contact with the legalistic God of the Jewish intelligentsia. His contact was with the living God who permeated the living memory of his people.

As a Galilean, Jesus grew up in contact with diverse peoples and cultures, yet far from all the "centers of belonging"—political, intellectual, or religious. Rejected and put down by all the in-groups of their world, the Galileans had learned through their margination and suffering to relativize society's absolutes. Relativizing human categories of importance and belonging, their one source of security was their deep faith in the God who alone was capable of salvation.

Jesus' identification with the most rejected of society and his love for them is one of the greatest constants of his ministry: it appears throughout the gospels and continues in the tradition of the church. Love and concern for the poor, the disfavored, and the oppressed of society is one of the most fundamental activities of the Christian group. In his continued identification with the poor and rejected of society, Jesus entered and left human society as a reject.

God's love for the rejected and his identification with them is brought out in the genealogy of Jesus according to Matthew (1:1-16). It begins with a converted pagan, Abraham, passes through the patriarchs, the slaves of Egypt, a shepherd who became king (David), and a carpenter (Joseph). Besides Mary his mother the other women mentioned include Tamar, who prostituted herself (Gen. 38:6-26), Ruth, who was a foreigner, Rahab, a harlot (Josh. 2:1), and the wife of Uriah who committed adultery with David (2 Sam. 11:4). When God entered into human history, he took it as it was. Neither racism, nor purity of blood, nor purity of morals, nor social class was respected in the incarnation. Matthew's genealogy puts Jesus very much among the out-groups.

Jesus is never identified as a scribe or a Pharisee, but it is evident that he knew scribes and Pharisees very well, and that he had mastered the Jewish traditions. Referred to as "Master" and as "Rabbi," he astounded even his enemies by his knowledge. Although he identified from the very beginning with the rejected, with the poor, simple, and the ignorant, and never appears to have lost the wisdom of the grass-roots populace, Jesus clearly appears to be more than just another "grass-roots" person or leader. He knew well the ways, the laws, and the traditions of the powerful of his time.

At a time when men considered it degrading to associate with women, Jesus had women in his company, even women who were possessed by evil spirits. He does not hesitate to praise the poor and condemn the rich (Luke 6:20-26). He praises the wisdom of the "simple people" in contradistinction to the wise and educated of this world (Matt. 11:25-30; Luke 10:21-23). He does not hesitate to eat with a Pharisee (Luke 7:36), but neither does he hesitate to call to his inner company one who was hated by both the poor and the rich alike: a tax collector (Matt. 9:9-13; Mark 2:13-17; Luke 5:27-32). He does not hesitate to eat at the same table with tax collectors and sinners, even when it scandalized others (Matt. 9:10-11).

His deep concern for the "little ones" of society is clearly brought out in Matthew 19:13-15, Mark 10:13-16, and Luke 18:15-17. He admonishes his followers that if they want to be truly great, they are to become "like the little ones" (Matt. 23:11; Mark 10:13-16; Luke 10:21-22). For Jesus, it is evident that the poor, the little ones, and the simple people—that is, all the classes considered inferior and tainted by society—will be the first ones to understand the love and the wisdom of the Father; the wise and intelligent of "this world" will be excluded. The sign of the new era will be that the poor will hear the good news; captives will be liberated; the blind will see; the oppressed will be liberated (Luke 4:18).

It is important to note that Jesus does not just *do things for* the poor, but he identifies with them in the most intimate way by being born one of them, learning from them, going to their homes, and eating with them. He is one of them, and he appears to feel comfortable in their company. On the other hand, he also appears to be comfortable with some others who were not popular with the common people, such as the tax collector, the Pharisee, and the rich government official named Zacchaeus (Luke 19:11).

What Kingdom?

At the time of Jesus great political unrest prevailed throughout Judea, and the Jews were expecting the Messiah to restore the kingdom. In the beginning, the proclamation of Jesus does not appear as new or radical. Israel had suffered great catastrophes—the breakdown of the kingdom, interior wars, exploitation by their own rich, captivity, exile, foreign domination. Yet through it all, Israel became more convinced that this could not be the final stage. Yahweh would come and triumph. If their God had delivered them from the pharaoh, he would do it again.

Jesus begins his preaching with the proclamation: "The time is fulfilled, and the kingdom of God is at hand; repent and believe in the gospel" (Mark: 1:15). For him the kingdom of God is not the apocalyptic end. It is a *beginning*—in this world. It was not the kingdom of judgment as announced by John the Baptist, which was to be ushered in through fasting and penance. It was not the kingdom of the Pharisees, which would come about by their manipulation of God through multiple "good and pious works." It was not the kingdom of the Zealots, which would be brought about by armed rebellion. Jesus proclaims the kingdom of the grace of God; not the kingdom of the vengeance of God.

Just what is this kingdom that will be the emphasis of the deeds and words of Jesus during his Galilean ministry? Into the kingdom of God, which is now beginning, Jesus invites all, especially those previously rejected by the existing social structures. If it would be hard for the rich, the righteous, and the powerful to enter, it would not be so much because of their wealth, righteousness, or power, but because, in their own way, they had made their own gods and on that basis looked down upon and despised others as inferior. Their gods determine their social status and prestige—not the God they name with their lips, but the gods who function in their hearts in determining the priorities of everyday life. In the kingdom, preached by Jesus, all are welcome without distinction.

The kingdom will begin within us when we accept God's offer of forgiveness and experience his unlimited love. When we have gone through such an experience we will forgive and love in the same way God has forgiven and loved us. This experience with the loving God will be the beginning of a new life within us (1 John 4). The greater our gratitude for what we have received, the greater will be our own generosity. Thus the kingdom will not be a new law telling us what we must do; it will be a new spirit enabling us to want to do much more than any law could command.

To appreciate the kingdom of God as lived and proclaimed by Jesus, it is necessary to go deeper into the ultimate identity of Jesus as lived and revealed by Jesus himself.

Who is this Jesus? There was something about him that was original, astonishing, and sometimes confusing. As believers today, we certainly know the fundamental reason for his fascinating originality: he was the Son of God. But how was this uniqueness manifested in his lifetime? What did others see and experience in him that was so totally different and appealing, even if it was sometimes scary?

It is clear from the gospels that Jesus exhibited an intimacy with God that was totally unheard of even to the Jewish people. This intimacy with God was at the very core of the uniqueness of Jesus. It is especially evident in the way he referred to God his Father, and taught his followers to imitate him in doing so.

The designation of God as Father is not unknown either to Judaism or to other religions. The Old Testament affirms that God is Father (Isa. 63:16; Jer. 3:4), but it never *invokes* God as Father. At the time of Christ, there were Jewish prayers in use that referred to God as "Our Father and Our King,"[8] but they never referred to him as "*my* Father," and they were spoken in Hebrew rather than in the ordinary language of the people. Jesus refers to God as "my father," which broke with all Jewish custom. But he went even further; he uses the Aramaic language and refers to God in a most intimate way: *Abba!* It was the very familiar term used by young

Westminster United Presbyterian Church
1501 WEST CLEVELAND Rᴅ.
SOUTH BEND, INDIANA 46628

children, and by adults, in addressing their own fathers. *Abba* is a very
childlike expression, comparable with the English "Dad" or "Daddy," or
with the Mexican-American *Papacito* or *Diosito.*

Jesus inaugurates a new relationship with God as Father inasmuch as he
makes it possible for others also to become sons and daughters of God
(John 1:12). He speaks about "my Father" (Matt. 15:13; 18:10), "your
Father," where the "your" is plural (Matt. 5:48; 10:29), "your Father,"
where the "your" is singular (Matt. 6:4, 18; John 20:17), and teaches his
followers to pray to "our Father" (Matt. 6:9–13; Luke 11:1–4). No one is
Father except God (Matt. 23:9). Jesus is the only Son (John 1:14); he is one ·
with the Father (John 10:30); he is sent by the Father (John 5:37–43); he has
learned from the Father and can reveal the Father's way to others (Matt.
11:27). In the Gospel of Luke, "Father" is in the first and the last phrase
that Jesus speaks (1:39; 23:46; cf. 24:49).

In this intimacy with God, Jesus also reveals a new anthropology: dignity,
confidence, security, docility, and self-respect based on freely chosen dependence on the one absolute: God. This unquestioned dependence on and
confidence in the one Absolute in turn frees his Followers from all other
humanly made absolutes or dependencies. It allows them to relate with each
other and with society in a radically new way.

Authority of Freedom

In his own public life, Jesus will live out the meaning and consequences of
this life of unquestioned dependency on and intimacy with God-*Abba.* As
we will see, intimacy with God does not remove his followers from the affairs and problems of the world. On the contrary, it plunges them into the
midst of everything that concerns society. Intimacy with God is not an escape from the world, but rather a deeper entry into the affairs of the world.

Out of this intimacy with God and submission to him come two related
ideas that appear throughout the gospels as characteristic of the way of
Jesus: his unquestioned authority and unlimited freedom.

The memory of the early Christians and the collective memory of Christians today picture Jesus as a man of unquestioned authority—though never
as authoritarian. The amazing thing is that the source of his authority appears to be in himself. When speaking, he does not appeal to the authority
of other texts or teachers: "you have heard it said . . . but I say to you"
(Mark 1:21–22; Matt. 7:28–29; Luke 4:31–32). The Sermon on the Mount is
filled with the spirit of "you have heard it said . . . but I say to you" (Matt.
5–7) and "at the end of the sermon, the crowds were astonished, because he
taught with authority and not like their scribes" (Matt. 7:28–29).

Furthermore, he has authority over sickness (Matt. 8:1–22; Luke 7:1–10),
over the elements of nature (Matt. 8:23–27), over devils (Matt. 8:28–34;
Luke 4:31–36), over sin (Matt. 9:1–8; Mark 2:1–12; Luke 5:17–26), and
over death (Matt. 9:18–26; Luke 7:11–17; 8:40–56). The crowds claim that

they have never seen such power in Israel, but the leaders, although not denying his power, attribute it to Satan (Matt. 9:33–34; Mark 2:12; Luke 5:26). This unschooled Galilean now amazed all with his wisdom and authority. It was authority as they had never experienced. It was the authority of God in the person of Jesus.

The other characteristic of Jesus that comes from his intimacy with God-*Abba* is his unlimited freedom. He allowed no person, tradition, or law to stand in his way of doing good to others, of loving them to the extreme, and of thus living out his mission from the Father. His unlimited freedom was a consequence of his total dependence and confidence in God-*Abba*.

In the story of Jesus in the temple at a tender age, he demonstrates a certain independence from his parents by staying in the temple. When his parents are astonished that he would do such a thing, the response is simple: "Did you not know that I had to be in my Father's house?" (Luke 3: 41–52).

The baptism of Jesus marks the turning point from his hidden life to his public mission. Jesus had assumed the total condition of his people. As the Epistle to the Hebrews puts it: "He had to become like his brothers in every way" (2:17). Jesus knows the sufferings of his people at the level of experiential knowledge for he has lived their sufferings, frustrations, and dreams, and made them his own. In his baptism, he began to express the meaning of his life and mission. Without ceasing to be one of the people, he leaves his family and home to take up his public mission. From this point on, Jesus no longer allows family and friends to keep him from doing what has to be done (Matt. 12:46–50; Mark 3:21, 31–35; Luke 8:19–21). His family will be those who keep the will of the Father.

It is evident from the temptation narratives (Luke 4:1–13) that Jesus rejects the temptations to possession of wealth, prestige, and power. He overcomes the temptations that entice some to want to have more, to want a more important position than others, and to want more power over others. Throughout the gospels, he appears to be quite free about being "socially acceptable" to any of the in-groups of his time. He is free to be himself and to speak, visit, and eat with whom he pleases. No social category of acceptability keeps him from doing what he feels has to be done (see Mark 2:16; Matt. 11:19). He freely mixes with *all!* The militant, the pious, the Pharisees, sinners, publicans, tax collectors—Jesus appears to have a total disregard for society's categories of "belonging."

He defies the categories of public opinion (Mark 2:13; Luke 5:27–32) by inviting a tax collector into his inner circle, defies socially accepted norms by questioning the decree on divorce (Mark 10:6), and appears free in choosing his friends—both men and women.

He is free of political pressures. When the politically powerful Herod wants to see him, he sends word: "Go tell that so-and-so" (Luke 13:32). When confronted by the representative of the most powerful man on earth, Caesar, he is not intimidated; he remains the master of the situation (John

18:28–19:22). But neither is he enslaved by the political activists of his day, the Zealots. It appears that Jesus was sympathetic and even friendly with them. It is the only group that is not clearly criticized in the gospels. Some of the disciples were certainly from this group (Simon the Zealot, Judas, and possibly Peter). Yet, although friendly with them and possibly even agreeing with them on some points, he does not tie himself down to their cause.

Jesus has close friends, as revealed throughout the gospels. Yet he never appears to be tied down by them. He is free from peer-pressure, which is often the strongest enslavement. The two sons of Zebedee are refused their ambitious desires (Mark 8:27–33); Peter is told to shut up and quit tempting him (Mark 8:27–33).

Jesus appears to be a prophet, but much more than a prophet (Mark 8:28; Matt. 21:11). Scholars today are more and more convinced that this was the most original title given to him by others. It is even more striking that the crowds see Jesus as a prophet at a time when it was unusual to think that someone was a prophet, much less *the* prophet. Jewish religion had become a religion of law and script, and there was no place for the disturbing element of prophecy. Prophecy appeared to be only for the lunatic fringe of society. In fact, after the fall of Jerusalem, there were rabbis who said that the gift of prophecy had been given only to lunatics. The nonscribal, charismatic, prophetic personality of Jesus, and also of John the Baptist, was a shock and provocation for the representatives of official Judaism. Just as the Grand Inquisitor of Dostoevski, they as much as asked him: "Why did you come to disturb us?"

Jesus often appears to be a rabbi, and is usually called a rabbi by those who do not believe in him. He has disciples whom he instructs, but they never become rabbis themselves. He teaches in the synagogues, but mostly in the open air. Among his audiences were persons whom an official rabbi would avoid: children, tax collectors, public sinners. Beyond all this, his manner of teaching differed profoundly from that of the other rabbis. The rabbis interpreted Scripture on the authority of previous authorities, but Jesus speaks on his own authority. He does not use complicated arguments, as the rabbis were prone to do, but the simple talk of the ordinary people. He speaks about experiences familiar to everyone, and he uses the established structure of tradition and sacred texts but without tying himself down to them.

In Matthew 15:1–20 it is evident that Jesus and his disciples were not too concerned with the sacred structures of determined acts and norms that had been set up and insisted upon by the scribes and Pharisees. They came to Jesus and asked him: "Why do your disciples act contrary to the traditions of our ancestors?" (Matt. 15:2) to which Jesus responded by condemning their traditions: "Why do you for your part act contrary to the commandment of God for the sake of your traditions?" (Matt. 15:3).

Jesus appears as the nonconformist who breaks with the tradition of the spiritual masters of his day who imposed many observances upon their disciples (Mark 2:18–22; Luke 5:33–39). He does not require fasting and penances in return for his time. Nor does he think that he has to escape to the desert in order to get away from the contaminated world. He does not separate himself from the ordinary people and even from the "shabby" characters of his society.

The primary liturgical imperative of Judaism is also relativized by Jesus. In Mark 2:23–28 and Luke 6:1–5 it is clear that, although not rejecting the sacred institution of the Sabbath, Jesus is not enslaved by it either. In his controversy with the Pharisees, he relativizes not only the Sabbath but the entire law: every institutionalized human practice is meant to serve human needs; if it is allowed to get in the way of doing good for others or to limit someone's capacity for helping others, it has outlived its purpose. "The Sabbath is made for man, not man for the Sabbath" (Mark 2:27).

At the time of Jesus, practically every human action was prescribed and determined by the law. The human conscience was not free; it was heavily burdened by an insupportable complex of legal prescriptions. In his very lifestyle and words, Jesus shows that he is not a slave to the law. Thanks to his oneness with the Spirit within, he enjoys a marvelous freedom from within the law. Jesus will not allow the law to get in the way of doing good to others.

The law had brought enslavement. Observance of the overburdening law had blinded persons to the needs of their fellow humans. The law had become a source of hostility and alienation. It had to be broken in order that men and women could be liberated to serve their neighbors.

Transcending the Dilemma of Acceptance/Rejection

To experience and recognize that the kingdom of God is the kingdom of our Father and that we as his children can be on intimate terms with this all-powerful God might at first reading appear naive and simplistic. Yet the reinterpretation of the symbol of the kingdom of God through the symbol of the intimacy of God-Abba will have world-shaking consequences for all subsequent history. The world as built by power games and exploitation comes to an end with the confrontation of God-Father present and active in our midst.

Even the most democratic of modern societies structure themselves on relationships of equality and inequality, superiority and inferiority, *and* think that such exclusivism was operative only in ancient times. At the time of Jesus, many jobholders—shepherds, barbers, medical practitioners, tax collectors, government workers (publicans)—were considered legally "unclean" and to mix with them would bring about a legal contamination. Although we do not speak about "unclean" professions today, the same kind of stereotype continues to operate. There are certain professions that persons gladly speak about and identify themselves or their friends with, but others are considered unworthy of polite, clean, ordinary society.

Jesus breaks with the standard respectable/trash, pure/impure, clean/
unclean, righteous/sinner categories of his society and of every society.
Nothing that comes from outside contaminates (Mark 7:15). He mixes
freely with all—men and women, adults and children, public sinners and
ordinary persons, Jews and foreigners. And who is his family? Not his
parents and relatives, but whoever does the will of the Father. And titles?
His followers are to have none, for God alone is superior. No humanly instituted category can be used as the basis for considering one person better or
worse than another. There *are* human differences, but in the kingdom of
God all are children of the same Father and all have an equal share in the
fundamental dignity of membership in the same family. Shared intimacy
with God is the basis for a new vision of all persons and therefore of new
social structures.

What counts in the kingdom of the Father is not the external titles and
labels that individuals attach to themselves and to others—pure, sinner,
solid citizen, outsider, educated, good-for-nothing. The only thing that
counts in the kingdom of the Father is what is revealed in the heart that
opens itself to God, and because it opens itself to God as our Father, it cannot help opening to other human beings who now appear, not as better or
worse, but as brothers and sisters. To accept God as Father is to accept my
total dependence upon his loving sovereignty and paternity. This is the only
criterion of belongingness. It was this new attitude of the followers of Jesus
that provoked without violence or political preaching a social and cultural
revolution within the Jewish religion, Hellenistic culture, and the Roman
Empire that continues to influence our world today. Its impact will continue
until the end of time.

In every first-party/other-party relationship, whether personal (I-you) or
group (we-they), the introduction of a third party will alter the relationship.
The third party can lead to an enriching experience: a friend of both
through whose presence both will come to know and appreciate each other
better. A mutual third party—a friend—of two who are enemies can open
the way for a deblocking of whatever makes them enemies, allowing them
to cross the boundaries of their polarizations. If the introduction of a third
party affects only one pole of the I-you or of the we-they relationship, it can
lead to division of the I-you/we-they relationships. If two are invited to
friendship with a third, but only one chooses to accept, jealousy and division can follow.

Jesus introduces a third term that can function in all human relationships:

You have heard it said, "love your neighbor . . . and hate your
enemy." But I say to you, love your enemies and pray for those who
persecute you, so that you may be sons of your father in heaven, who

makes the sun to rise over the good and the evil and sends his rain over the just and the unjust [Matt. 5:43–45].

Because Christian love is based on the common relationship of all, without exception, it can know no barriers of caste, class, citizenship, religion, ideology, parenthood, or whatever. The basis of the new belonging and acceptability is the recognition and acceptance of the common fatherhood of God. Regardless of our too human relationships of acceptance or rejection, we are now interrelated through a third other who immediately opens new possibilities to bypass the normal acceptance-rejection dynamics of group or personal relationships.

Jesus lives and offers to us the opportunity of breaking through the sin of the world—structures and boundaries of rejection—by accepting that we are all children of the same God-*Abba*. A new common element is introduced into the universal human adventure. New, not because the presence and knowledge of God's working through human history would be something new, especially to the Jewish people, but new because it revealed something radically new about the nature of human persons—their inherent dignity as children of God, and as brothers and sisters to one another. As such, everyone is called to cooperate with God in his plans for the world, not as superiors and inferiors, but as children and friends.

It is the new relationships through a third person—God-*Abba*—that allows us to break through the exploitor-exploited dialectic and form a new partnership. Thus there are not the dominant who can afford to be charitable to the dominated—and in being charitable continue to dominate and dehumanize—but neither is there a role change whereby the dominated now become the dominant. There must be a restructuring from a bipolar to a tripolar model of relationship.

The third other offers the possibility of a new "us." Through the third other, the "we" (dominant) and the "they" (dominated) will be able to see each other in a new way—in what they really are as human beings and not as masked, stereotyped, or categorized by society. In the new "us" certain differences will continue but they will be seen in a new way—not in terms of exploitor-exploited, master-slave, civilized-savage, superior-inferior, but in terms of interdependence and cooperation of all in a common undertaking for the benefit of all.

Such a change is a threat to all those who have built their own personal security and prestige on the basis of an "*I* versus *you*" or "*we* versus *they*" polarization. In such a society, "we," the powerful and established, can be very charitable to "them," the poor, ignorant, backward . . . but they remain "they" and are never allowed to become "us."

Because Jesus introduces humanity to a new model of human existence that destroys the earthly basis of segregation, another kind of division will come about. Those who cannot accept a universal belonging and who insist on the maintenance of segregative barriers will not only refuse the invitation to join the new group, but will fight actively to discredit and oppose it. Those with a comfortable and well defined earthly existence will resist. The powerful, established, prestigious, and privileged will fight against the new way. One constant easily discovered in the gospels is that the wise and the powerful of this world will exclude themselves from the kingdom. They too are invited, but seldom accept (Luke 14:13-21).

The kingdom of the Father offers a new *basis* for any given society—that is, it does not offer (merely) a new social *system* or *ideology*. The followers of Jesus will constitute a new human *group*, not merely another human *structuring*. This recognizable group will function throughout all human structures. It will even help to formulate and introduce new structures, knowing well that new life can never be reduced to any one human structure.

Like any other human group, it will have easily recognizable features: the "language" of the group might best be summarized in the Our Father; the members are from all classes and all ethnic backgrounds; their lifestyle is best described in the life of radical love and forgiveness spelled out in the Sermon on the Mount; their most distinctive cultic rite is the festive and joyous banquet proclaiming the memory of the founder. By that which is most original to them—the newness and uniqueness of universal fellowship under God-*Abba*—they will shine forth and be a new light to all peoples and all social structures. This new light will be good news to some and judgment to others.

The restructuring that flows from the mutual acceptance of the third other will have religious, intellectual, economic, and social implications for a new worldview—that is, the culture of a group and of its relations with other groups. To really believe and proclaim the fundamental Christian symbol that Jesus was crucified and resurrected because he dared to live and proclaim the full implications of "our Father" as the fundamental basis of humanizing and liberating society is not only to restructure oneself, but also to work for the restructuring of one's world.

For the nonwhite peoples of the world, the white has generally been the dominant enemy; and for the white, the nonwhite has generally been the threat to whiteness as normative for all. Only a deep trust in our mutual Father will allow us to bypass the deeply engrained segregative racial blockage in order to see, appreciate, and love racial and cultural differences as mutually contributory to the building of the kingdom. Each person and each group has its share of richness to offer to the others, and each its own share of poverty to be alleviated by the others. It is in this freely accepted relationship of interdependence and mutual cooperation that the kingdom of the children of God emerges from within the kingdoms of this world.

Although some will accept this tripolar relationship, others will reject not only it, but also those who accept it. The new model of human existence will be opposed by those who would rather maintain their bipolar, segregative models. This will bring about hatred, division, and persecution between those who accept the new way and those who hold on to the old way that insists on divisions and segregative differences as the basis of human survival (see Matt. 10:16–39).

The Galilean Crisis:
Symbol of the Rupture That Inaugurates Liberation

From the beginning of the public ministry of Jesus, it is evident that his followers were enthusiastic about what he was doing and saying, yet it is equally evident that from the very beginning they likewise had difficulty accepting and understanding his ways, especially in the light of their laws, customs, and traditions. What he said appeared too good to be true. Even the disciples do not comprehend the extent of what he is trying to tell them (Mark 7:18; Matt. 15:16). The weight of their traditions blinds them from fully understanding and appreciating the liberating way of Jesus.

The most basic tenet of their Jewish faith was that God would intervene in history in their behalf. Through the gradual accumulation of multiple laws, customs, and traditions, the God who is sovereign and who saves freely had come to appear as the God who had to be manipulated or coerced by rituals and observances if he was to act in their behalf. The people firmly believed that God would come and restore their kingdom. On this hope and expectation all were united but they differed as to how this expectation was to be achieved. The Pharisees thought it would come about through their observance of the law; the Essenes through their absolute purification and the living of the law in an ideal state; the Zealots through armed rebellion. They differed in the means of achievement, but there was no doubt that the kingdom was for the chosen people.

Jesus started preaching that the expected kingdom was now to begin. He spoke their language and started from their traditions. Yet from the very beginning he begins to break with many of their traditions. Every "tradition" that was supposed to be a way of forcing the kingdom to come is questioned or transgressed by Jesus—the purity laws, the pious practices, the religious observances. He openly breaks with the traditions that were supposed to usher in the kingdom, yet he openly proclaims that the kingdom is coming—the time of expectation has been fulfilled.

In breaking with their traditions, Jesus disappoints everyone. Even Peter rebukes him for speaking about a suffering Messiah (Matt. 16:22). Jesus breaks with their expectations not by going *against* them, but by going completely *beyond* them. He does not replace one system of enslavement by another, but rather goes to the root causes of the enslavement of any system: the deification of the system and of human effort to maintain the system. The Jewish system, like every other human system, tended to absolutize and exclusivize itself, making of itself an absolute end. While rejecting "foreign gods," their own laws, rituals, and traditions had, in effect, become gods. The living God who liberates had been replaced in practice by laws and rituals that in the name of God enslaved the people.

Jesus does not proclaim a structureless society, but he does question the deification of any and every human structuring. Even though structures are needed, no structure can substitute for the spirit that gave rise to the structures. The more the structures hide or obscure the originative spirit, the more they will be enslaving and dehumanizing rather than liberating and life-giving.

In breaking with their traditional structures and expectations, precisely in order to welcome all the rejected into the kingdom, Jesus ends up being rejected by his own people. He who has begun the practice of inviting all and rejecting no one is now rejected because he has not conformed to what was expected of him.

The people wanted a new structure (the restoration of the kingdom), and Jesus will not give them what they want; instead he will give them a new spirit that will stand in judgment on all structures. He must break with their expectations in order to bring about what they desire at a still deeper level, but do not even know how to conceptualize—the true freedom of the children of God—as easily happens with every religious tradition.

The geographical break with Galilee is symbolic of Jesus' break with the traditions that were in effect enslaving the people while proclaiming the one God who liberates. Mark 7:1-24 brings this out very clear. "You have pushed aside the commandment of God in order to implant your tradition" (Mark 7:9). The people and his own disciples do not understand: "Are you, too, incapable of understanding?" (Mark: 7:18). "Jesus left there and went to the region of Tyre" (Mark 7:24). This is the moment of crisis; Jesus "breaks" with Galilee and goes to a pagan region of racial and religious mixture (Mark 7:24–8:10). The break is definite and its meaning will gradually become clearer: the expected kingdom has started, but not in accordance with their expectations. Thus there is continuity (the kingdom has started) but there is also radical break or transcendence (the kingdom is something radically beyond their expectations). It will be a more expansive salvation and liberation than they had even dreamed of or expected. Furthermore it will come about in a totally unsuspected way.

The Galilean crisis marks one of the crucial moments of the continuity/transcendence that is so characteristic of the entire way of Jesus. In breaking with their *traditions*, Jesus does not destroy *tradition*, but *reaffirms* the strongest and most original element of it: there is only one living God and nothing can take the place of this God. By *breaking* with traditions that function as gods, he *reaffirms* the one God.

Chapter 5

FULFILLMENT IN JERUSALEM

*From then on Jesus began to
indicate to his disciples that he
must go to Jerusalem
[Matt. 16:21].*

Throughout much of their history, the Israelites had been a conquered people. They had come from slavery in Egypt, to the wandering in the desert, and finally to the promised land. Their build-up as a nation was carried out by Saul, David, and Solomon. They went through inner divisions, the Babylonian exile, and finally, by the time of Jesus, they had found themselves again in the promised land but under the domination of the Roman empire. Generally speaking, they were scorned by the Gentile world because of their fanatic religious convictions and practices.

This struggling group of nomadic tribes had managed to reach the land promised to them by God, captured it and even managed to take over the holy city of Jerusalem where they installed the ark of the covenant, built a great temple to house Yahweh's presence, and a great palace for their kings. Having often been deprived of a national territory of their own, hope for the land became one of the fundamental drives of the Jewish people. And because God had chosen them out of all the peoples of the world, their land seemed to them the very center of the earth. In the very center of the city was the temple—the innermost core of Jewish existence. There the ark of the covenant stood until 587 B.C. (Ezek. 38:12 and 5:5). In Jerusalem the Jews felt at home within the ordered universe of their worldview and beliefs.

Jerusalem had been chosen by Yahweh to become his throne (Jer. 3:16–17). For the prophet Ezekiel, the ark and the temple may pass away, but the presence of Yahweh continues to be the heart of the holy city (Ezek. 48:38). When even the temple was destroyed, Jerusalem remained the holy center of Judaism. The destruction in 587 was a national trauma and it forced them to rethink their ecclesiology as a people. The wisdom literature is an example of their efforts to survive as a people even in the Diaspora. Certain religious institutions not directly related to the temple—the Torah, the Sabbath, and the synagogue—became new rallying points. But the post-exilic restoration and the apocalyptic dreams of a new and final temple also continued to hold them together. It was their religious symbol that guaranteed their continuity and their hope for liberation. It is a great tribute to the Jewish people that in spite of the many invasions, exiles, and persecutions, they maintained their identity as a people.

Their religion became their main source of identity, unity, and protection against the military and cultural powers that threatened to destroy them as a people. The all-important role of religion helps us to understand why the leaders became so absolutist about the one thing that held them together as a people: their tradition. For many it was their love for their people as a people that made them unbending in their ways. By the time of Jesus, tradition had been absolutized and dogmatized in such a way that it then functioned more as an imposition, as a heavy burden, and even as a curse. It no longer appeared as a gift of God in the service of the people. While some imposed the traditions out of sincerity, others took advantage of them as a source of profit and security through exploitation of the weaker. In either case, the God who intervenes in history in behalf of his people had come to be understood as the uncompromising God who makes burdensome demands. These absolutized traditions had hidden and even perverted the original tradition—as easily happens with every religious tradition.

Jerusalem: Symbol of Established Power

Why did Jesus have to go to Jerusalem? From the perspective of the Old Testament and the expectations of the Jewish people, there appears to be no doubt that Jesus *had* to go to Jerusalem to bring about salvation. That salvation would begin in Jerusalem appears to be one of the basic tenets of the Jewish faith at the time of Jesus. Jerusalem and everything about it was heavy with religious significance: it was the holy city of the people of God; it was the site of the temple; it was the subject of much of the prophetic literature; it was the center of Jewish identity and belonging; it was the designated place of God's abiding presence. Yet, since Jesus consistently moved in unsuspected directions, could there have been other unsuspected reasons why Jesus had to go to Jerusalem to initiate the definitive reign of God among all persons?

From the perspective of the base of Jewish society we can see another reason why Jesus had to go to Jerusalem: it was the center of the powers that excluded and oppressed the masses. Jesus had to attack oppression at its very roots. He had to go to the roots of the power structures. For us, Jerusalem stands as the symbol of absolutized power that cloaks the crimes of the powerful in multiple ways—and worst of all, it does it in the name of God! Galilee, as we have seen, was a marginated region outside the centers of power. The Galilean *has* to go to Jerusalem. It is this very tension between Galilee and Jerusalem that, culturally speaking, appears to be the dynamic core of the liberating and salvific "way of Jesus." It was not just the death on the cross that was salvific, but the entire way that climaxed on the cross. It is in the conflictual tensions of the way from Galilee to Jerusalem that the full impact of the salvific way of Jesus emerges. It is not so much Jerusalem alone that is the focal point of Jesus' salvific way, as the tension between Galilee (marginal existence) and Jerusalem (established existence).

As the site of the temple, Jerusalem had become the center of religious domination. The clergy, especially the high clergy, regulated the multiple purification rituals that dominated the practice of Jewish religion. These multiple and complex rituals were imposed upon the people as a means of cleansing themselves from the many "stains and contaminations" that had been determined by the priests and the intellectuals of the time. Whoever could not come to the temple to offer the necessary purification rituals was considered to be legally impure.

Jerusalem was also the site of the greater rabbinical schools where Jews went to study so that eventually they could become "doctors." The scribes—that is, the degreed intellectuals—considered themselves to have a monopoly on knowledge and its power. They alone were the authorized interpreters of the law. They dominated the masses through a type of intellectual moralism inasmuch as they imposed their knowledge as God's way.

Along with these degreed intellectuals, there were the enlightened laymen who were the Pharisees. They too had sought to liberate Judaism from the clergy, but had succeeded only in introducing a new type of domination for, along with the scribes, they looked down upon the religion of the ordinary people as uninformed and impure. Whoever was ignorant of the law could not keep it, and if one could not keep the law, one had sinned. The ignorant were sinners.

Jerusalem was also the center of economic, political, and military domination. It was the gathering site of the great merchants, landowners, and growers. The dominant ruling class cooperated with the Roman authorities in maintaining the status that favored their own money-making interests. Besides the foreign military power, the local ruling class was composed of the priestly nobility and the rich property owners who were called "the ancients" and, along with some scribes who were chiefly from the Pharisaical party, together made up the Sanhedrin. Under the Roman procurators, it was the chief governing body of the land. Thus the higher clergy, educators, and businessmen ruled over the people. Cooperation with Rome meant a peaceful continuation of life and commerce. Much of the commerce of Jerusalem was tied in with its being the site of the temple and therefore the destination of many religious pilgrimages. Being at the religious center of Judaism was in itself good business: travelers and pilgrims had need of food, clothing, and shelter. The provision of victims for the prescribed sacrifices was another good business.

There were great divisions and hatreds among the Pharisees, who stressed the law, the Sadducees, who stressed the temple, and the wealthy who were primarily interested in their own wealth and whatever might protect their interests. If Jerusalem was the center of Palestinian Judaism and of the unity of the Jewish people, it was also the center of deep-rooted religious divisions and hatreds. It was the center of unreconcilable polarizations: each group believed itself to be in possession of the absolute truth.

In Jerusalem we see how institutions set up to help the people—the law and the temple—in turn become absolutized and self-serving. Institutions necessary for group existence also become the source of collective blindness. It is this institutional blindness that allows well meaning persons to destroy others while thinking they are doing good and even serving God. It is the structural make-up of society, when absolutized, that destroys human dignity by making persons serve the institutions rather than helping the institution to serve human needs.

Jerusalem can be seen as a symbol of the structural absolutism that sacralizes divisions, rejection of others, and even hatred and murder—all in the name of God. It is symbolic of the triple domination of the masses: religious (elitism based on cultic practices), intellectual (elitism based on moralistic knowledge), and politico-economico-military (elitism based on power, wealth, and collaboration with the Roman empire). All three forms of domination and oppression, while not appearing to work together intentionally, nevertheless worked together in practice to the complete rejection, exploitation, and oppression of the poor and the simple. In contemporary terms, we could say that the church leadership, the academic community, and "the pillars of the community" worked together in the ongoing domination of the base of society.

The Ultimate Struggle: Spirit versus Establishment

The Reject who Rejects Rejection

From the very beginning of his public life, Jesus astonished everyone. He was a "second-class citizen" with no formal studies. He was the son of a carpenter from Nazareth. He was a "yokel," an upstart—a Galilean reject—yet he astounded not only the masses but likewise the leaders of the people (Mark 3:22, 7:1). He astounded them with his knowledge and wisdom, and he shocked them with his actions.

Jesus proclaimed intimacy with God-*Abba* as a central facet of the kingdom of God. He shared table-fellowship with tax collectors and public sinners—and even said that it was a sign that the kingdom was indeed beginning.

His attitude of welcoming the rejected is brought out again and again in his parables: the parable of the lost sheep, the lost coin, the prodigal son, the great supper, the Pharisee and the tax collector, the good Samaritan, and others. The very ones who were commonly thought to be the proof of moral reprobation are now treated as privileged guests.

Jesus did not simply *proclaim* this attitude, he lived it himself, and in such a way that it was said of him that he was himself a "glutton and drunkard" (Matt. 11:16–19). As Perrin points out, the scriptural wording could be an illusion to the fact that his table-fellowship with the rejects of Jewish society was not merely a polite get-together, but a friendly and joyous occasion where the guests truly enjoyed themselves.

The practices and teachings of Jesus struck a heavy blow at the fundamental convictions of the Jewish people of the time. He appeared to prostitute everything that the Jewish establishment had come to hold as sacred and that had become the basis for the survival and salvation of the people. Jewish authorities had worked hard to keep the community whole and pure. Now, in the name of the same God and kingdom, the unauthorized Galilean was challenging the very basis of the theological edifice that crowned their theocratic endeavors.

Jesus knew from personal experience how the various codes of "purity" of the different power groups dominated and oppressed his people. In his public activity, he begins to destroy the various fibers that made up the symbolic tissue of the "purity code" of his society. Clevenot states:

> All these practices of Jesus had in common the refusal of the magic attitude in relation to the agonizing death which was present in the crowds—fever, leprosy, paralysis. . . . The system of purity had as its purpose the exorcism of this violence through the magic of the sacrifices of the temple and the scrupulous observation of the law. But this system, designed and governed by the dominant class, had as its primary objective the maintenance of this domination.[1]

Through his actions, Jesus forces the hidden violence of the system out into the open. This could be done only by confronting the structures that claimed to exorcise violence while in fact perpetuating it. The exorcists of violence must now be exorcised themselves. Through these confrontations, the full identity of Jesus will be made known to his disciples: the Messiah, yes, but a suffering Messiah who will be rejected and crucified for his people.

In his own home territory Jesus appears to have failed, for in the end he is rejected by his own people. It is not enough to work among the people, making them aware of their fundamental dignity and worth. He had to go to the source—the center—of the problem. To eliminate rejection, he had to go to Jerusalem (Luke 9:52; Matt. 16:21).

The Galilean crisis and the confession of Peter mark a definite transition in the public ministry of Jesus. Having left Galilee to go to Jerusalem, Jesus poses the key question to his disciples: "Who do the others say that I am?"

And "Who do *you* say that I am?" (Matt. 16:13-21; Mark 8:27-31; Luke 9:18-22). Peter's response is well known: "You are the Messiah." Jesus does not deny that he is the Messiah, but he immediately begins to tell them about his future: he has to suffer much, and be rejected by the elders, the priests, and the intellectuals (scribes).

It is evident from the text that Peter does not approve of the reference to the suffering Messiah. He had recognized him as the Messiah, but in his own mind it was most probably a Messiah of conquest and power, who would restore the earthly kingdom. This was a definite temptation for Jesus himself: "Get behind me, Satan, you are a danger to me because you do not think of the things of God, but of human things" (Matt. 16:23). Jesus knows that when he confronts the power structures he will be destroyed by them, yet he also knows that it is the only way to triumph definitively over evil (Matt. 16:21).

After this declaration about the suffering Messiah, Jesus begins to call his followers not simply to a table-fellowship, but to take up their cross and follow him on his way. This invitation appears as a complete contradiction to everything they had expected about the kingdom. He not only invites them to take up their cross and follow him, but he likewise invites them to forget themselves in order to save themselves—forget yourself for the sake of Jesus and the good news and you will find yourself, but if you seek yourself, you will lose yourself. This was the very opposite of the way of the Pharisees, the scribes, and the priests (Matt. 24:24-28; Mark 8:34-38; Luke 9:23-27, 18:34). Even the apostles did not understand what Jesus was speaking about.

The disciples of Jesus cannot be content with welcoming others and doing good for others. They must join him in his struggle against the root and multiple causes of oppression. It is not sufficient to do good and avoid evil: the disciple must do good and *struggle against* evil. This is not an easy task, and it is evident from the New Testament that part of Jesus did not want to go through with it (Luke 22:42), but he realized that he had no choice if his mission from the Father was to be accomplished.

Man Confronts the Sacred

In the synoptic gospels, Jesus' ministry in Jerusalem centers around the temple: upon his arrival he goes to the temple; it is there that he teaches openly, to the great amazement of the people and the indignation of the various power blocs. To question and challenge the use of the temple was to challenge official Judaism at its very roots.

The tradition of the tension between Jesus and the temple is elaborated in various ways by the authors of the gospels: Jesus speaks about the destruction of the temple (Mark 13:2); the allegations before Caiaphas (Matt. 26:61; Mark 14:58) and the ridiculing at the cross (Matt. 27:39; Mark 15:29) are based on what his accusers maintain he had said about the temple.

Finally there was the rupture of the temple veil at the death of Jesus (Matt. 27:51). What Jesus said about the temple is brought into the trial of Stephen (Acts 6:14). The tension between Jesus and the temple is one of the key tensions in the gospels.

The expulsion of the merchants from the temple is a symbolic action placed by the synoptics in the final week of the life of Jesus. Thus it is linked intimately to the condemnation of Jesus, in which the idea of the destruction of the temple plays a key role. John places the cleansing of the temple toward the beginning of the public ministry (John 2:13–22) and makes it a much more violent attack upon the temple than it is in the synoptics. By making it such a strong attack, he links it with the mounting tensions between Jesus and the establishment, which led to his death. The symbolic action of Jesus is directed against the reality and the theology of the temple. It appears undeniable that there was a preresurrection tradition of tension between Jesus and the temple.

Jesus enters the courtyard at the moment when it is filled with pilgrims. He attacks the system of buying and selling, and justifies his action by appealing to the Old Testament:

> My house will be called a house of prayer for all the peoples, but you have made it a robbers' den [Mark 11:17; see also Matt. 21:12–13; Luke 19:45–46; John 2:13–22].

It is important to note that two Old Testament texts have here been fused into one. The first part is taken from Isaiah 56:7 "My house will be called a house of prayer for all peoples." It was an announcement of universalism and the end to all types of exclusivism or particularism—no one shall be excluded from Yahweh, for Yahweh is the God of all peoples. But the temple officials had devised ways of excluding many, even some of their own, from entry into the temple. Instead of being a house of prayer for all peoples, it had become a barrier that kept many away from God. It had become the opposite of what it should be and the authorities were maintaining it that way.

The second part of the citation comes from Jeremiah 7:9–11:

> Are you to steal and murder, commit adultery and perjury, burn incense to Baal, go after strange gods that you know not, and yet come to stand before me in this house which bears my name, and say: "We are safe; we can commit all these abominations again"? Has this house which bears my name become in your eyes a den of thieves?

In this prophecy Jeremiah condemns religion that masks exploitation of others for self-gain, that sacralizes and legitimizes the aggression and violence of the powerful, and that "purifies" externally while injustices continue.

In his condemnation of the merchants, Jesus condemns the whole temple theology by fusing two prophetic oracles in such a way that they interpret each other. The destruction of the temple, which had become a place to disguise the ongoing injustices of an in-group (Jer. 7:14–15), is joined with its being opened up to all peoples (Isa. 56:1–8). The destruction of the temple will destroy the particularisms canonized by the system. No human institution, no matter how sacred it is held to be, can be allowed to serve as a "cover-up" or justification for injustices. The truth of humankind's sinfulness and violence, and of God's forgiving mercy, must be accessible to all.

Jesus touches the most sensitive nerves of Jewish society by bringing out into the open the perversion of the temple and its leaders. In Israel, God alone was supreme and the leaders of the people were mandated to protect the people, especially the more defenseless, such as widows, orphans, and aliens (Jer. 7:1–7). The temple, the visible sign of God's saving presence, was supposed to be the guarantee that God was acting on behalf of his people. But God's way had been perverted. The leaders, far from protecting the defenseless, had become their exploiters and they used the temple to cloak their wrong doing.

The New Priesthood

The powerful are afraid of Jesus now because he has the masses behind him. It will not be easy to get rid of him. So his credibility has to be destroyed. The establishment—consisting of the chief priests, the scribes, and the elders—confronts him in the temple and demands of him: "By what authority are you doing these things? Who gave you this authority to do them?" (see Matt. 21:23–27; Mark 11:27–33; Luke 20:1–8). They attempt to destroy his credibility by presenting difficult questions, but the responses of Jesus consistently escape their traps. Not being able to destroy his credibility, they decide to destroy the prophet himself (see Matt. 14:1–2, 26:1–5; Luke 22:1–2; John 11:47, 49, 53).

The power structures can allow a popular leader some leeway while they plot and plan carefully. Once the decision is made to eliminate the threat, a way will be found and public opinion will be shaped to go along with and support it. The high priest makes the decision: "It is better that one should die than that the nation should perish" (John 11:50).

Jesus must die because he had exposed the establishment for what it was: a self-serving group exploiting the masses under the disguise of serving them and—worse yet—exploiting them in the name of offering sacrifice to Yahweh. Sacrifice had always been a part of the Jewish religion, and the early Christians would later continue their sacrifices at the temple. The sacrificing of surrogate victims is also questioned by Jesus. He brings out the true idea of perfect sacrifice in Mark 8:37: "What can a man give as a substitute for himself?" Such a statement hits at the very core of the system of vicarious sacrifices. The true sacrifice, which alone is pure adoration of

God, is the giving of one's life for the sake of others. It is in this light that we touch on Jesus' own understanding of his passion and death. Substitute victims or offerings can never equal the gift of oneself.

The Father willed the redemption of humankind through love even at the cost of the life of his only-begotten Son. And Jesus was lovingly obedient to his Father—not only unto death, but even to death on the cross (Phil. 2:6ff).

It is in this light that we can best appreciate the celebration of the last supper, the institution of the Christian priesthood, and the eucharistic sacrifice. The free offering of oneself for the sake of others is the bread of life. In his typical simplicity, Jesus takes the most ordinary and fundamental staples of nourishment: bread and wine. This bread—blessed, broken, and given to others—is his very body given for the sake of humanity. This wine—blessed and given to others—is his very blood for the new life of the world.

Rejection and Abandonment

Jesus freely offers his life, and the authorities seek to put him to death as a criminal guilty of subversion. In the crucifixion of Jesus, the powers of darkness certainly seem to triumph. In the New Testament accounts of his trial and passion no mention is made of anyone's having protested his condemnation. Judas, after having betrayed him, is the only one to publicly proclaim the innocence of Jesus (Matt. 27:3ff).

The final moments of the life of Jesus are astounding: he is betrayed by one of his own, abandoned by his closest friends—"and they all deserted him and fled" (Matt. 14:50) —condemned by the elite of his own people (Sanhedrin) and, in the name of the same God whom he proclaimed, handed over by them to the pagan authorities, and finally condemned by his own people. The whole crowd cried out, "Away with this man . . . crucify him" (Luke 23:18, 21). Even Peter, the spokesman of the group, explicitly denies that he knew him. Though the fourth gospel mentions that Jesus' mother, the sister of his mother, Mary the wife of Clophas, Mary Magdalene, and the beloved disciple stood near the cross (John 19:25–26), it is clear from the gospel tradition as a whole that nobody stood up to openly defend Jesus or to protest his condemnation.

All appear to reject Jesus and join in his condemnation—some actively and others passively; some vociferously and others in silence. God himself seems to withdraw his presence. Jesus, who had come to usher in the kingdom of universal fellowship, goes to his death alone, apparently rejected by everyone, God included.

Yet, in keeping with the image of the suffering servant of the Old Testament, Jesus neither condemns nor rejects anyone. As a true prophet he had exposed openly and clearly the abuses that had become ingrained in the traditions of his people. What he had to do, he did with compassion

Westminster United Presbyterian Church
1501 WEST CLEVELAND RD.
SOUTH BEND, INDIANA 46628

and love. Jesus weeps over Jerusalem for he truly loves the holy city of his people. He would have liked nothing better than to be able to say that everything was as it should be—but that would have been a betrayal of his people.

In his abandonment Jesus remains faithful to his convictions, to the very end. He surrenders his earthly life in distress but not in despair. He dies praying the psalm of a distressed but believing Jew: "My God, my God, why have you abandoned me?" God appears to have abandoned him. But Jesus does not abandon God! In his very recourse to Psalm 22 in his hour of supreme distress, he confesses his unwavering confidence in the God who will intervene in his behalf and in behalf of the defenseless and powerless (see Mark 14:34; Matt. 27:46).

If this unwavering confidence in God and his refusal to condemn anyone are implicitly brought out in Matthew and Mark, they are explicitly brought out in Luke, who puts the words of forgiveness as the first words of the crucified Jesus: "Father, forgive them for they know not what they do" (Luke 23:34) and ends his earthly existence with the words of total confidence: "Father, into your hands I commend my spirit" (Luke 23:46). Jesus is the free man who will not be forced by anyone or anything to be unfaithful to his convictions. All appear to have broken their relationship with him, but he breaks with no one. He remains in loving communion with everyone to the very end. Others might have abandoned him, but he abandons no one. Others condemn him, he condemns no one. Others lost faith in him (see Mark 14:15), but he loses faith in no one. In spite of everything, he remains in loving communion with everyone to the very end. He passes through human death in the absolute certainty that the Father will intervene in his behalf.

In his freely accepted death for the sake of life, Jesus redeemed the world from its self-destructive sinfulness. In the death and resurrection of Jesus, objective redemption has taken place. Its full implications will be better understood when the message and impact of the gospels make their way through time and space.

In his very defeat, he has been victorious. In destroying him the establishment confirmed the absolute truth of his accusations against it. The drama of Jerusalem is not only redemptive in itself, it is also symbolic of the drama of every human group that attempts to survive by its own power, by absolutizing its culture and its religion—in the conviction that its life, as seen by itself, is *the way* for everyone. In so doing, the group closes itself off from the infinite and from liberative growth. In absolutizing the "now" the group tends to forget the reason why it struggled and fought in order to have a new existence of its own.

"Our way," as we see it here and now, becomes our new idol—our own golden calf—which is not adored in words, but certainly in the daily deeds of life. It is these absolutized norms, values, and ideas that function as God and hide the real face of the living God.

Once a group has been victorious and has become established, it tends to forget the reasons behind the original violence that it fought against, which brought it into existence. It is willing to inflict the same violence on others in order to protect its institutions. Its own established way does not appear as violence to those in power, but as legitimate law and order for the sake of the common good. The great tragedy is that the "common good" usually tends to be identified with the self-interests of those who control society. They pass laws so that no one will do unto them as they have done unto others. By applying the laws of the institution, they kill the same prophetic voice that merely proclaims today what the original prophets of the group—the national heroes to whom monuments are built—proclaimed in the beginning. The very evils that the group had fought against have now become its own. To the degree to which the historical context and culture of the heroes is covered over, the very evil that they struggled against will be hidden and, worse yet, repeated by the very society that these sacrifices gave birth to. The very same prophetic voice that at one time was the word of liberation, now is heard as the word of judgment. Because no society likes to be judged as evil, its only recourse is to silence the disturbing voice.

This is why the authorities did not hesitate to kill Jesus. He had challenged them to be true to the very reason why they had been called into existence. He had dared to unmask the perversions that had invaded their sacred laws and traditions. He had to be destroyed.

Jerusalem reveals the drama of a people that begins to play God and is therefore convinced that to question it is to question God, to oppose it is to oppose God. It reveals the violence and ugliness of the rejection of others in the name of God. The cross reveals the worst side of religious conviction: murder of others in the name of God—crime masked as divine obligation, violence and aggression released through religious righteousness.

The Triumph of Nonviolence

There will be no human monument for Jesus—only an empty tomb—for Jesus dies in apparent defeat. But in fact he triumphed over violence without giving in to violent ways. He confronted violence with dynamic nonviolence—the only power that can change not only external structures but human hearts as well. The real monument to Jesus is the gospels, which attest not to a heroic call to arms and military conquest, but to his free offering of himself into the hands of his assassins. The nonviolence of Jesus is neither resignation nor passivity. It is the refusal to resign himself to evil. It is the power of his personal witness that reveals the violence and aggression of the violent to themselves and to everyone else. In the face of nonviolent witness, they can no longer hide their institutionalized crimes from themselves or from anyone else. They are defeated not through violence but through the power of truth: "You will know the truth, and the truth will set you free" (John 8:32).

The Sundered Temple Veil:
Symbol of the End of All Particularisms

The closing of the curtain usually marks the end of a performance. But the very opposite happens at the end of the earthly life of Jesus—the curtain is ripped open never to be closed again! The whole life of Jesus had been spent in guiding others to the truth. Jesus revealed the truth about persons in terms of God and the truth about God in terms of persons. Henceforth, all human knowledge is to be judged by this truth. In the light of this truth, nothing that dehumanizes or destroys human persons and society can be kept hidden and everything that truly humanizes and liberates persons and society will be exalted. At the end of the life of Jesus, the curtains that hide the truth are now opened forever, and no level of human knowledge will be left unaffected.

Jesus ends his earthly existence not in despair but with a loud cry of victory. The evangelists record that the curtain of the temple veiling the holy of holies was rent from top to bottom at the moment of his death. Just when the authorities thought that they had silenced him forever, the holy of holies is exposed and made accessible to everyone, even to non-Jews.

With the death of Jesus the curtain of the temple is sundered. The whole life of Christ had been a process of destroying all humanly made barriers that hindered free access to God-Father. Now, in his death, the final barrier is destroyed. There is no longer a division between priest and worshiper, for everyone is invited to join a priestly people; the division between Jew and Gentile is gone, for everyone now has free access to God. No human being has a privileged access to God, for all persons, because they are who they are, have the same access to God (Eph. 2:11-22). This marks the definitive end of all particularisms based on human criteria.

Now, when all the masks are removed and things appear for what they really are, the ultimate violence of domination and rejection in the name of God is fully revealed.

> And when the centurion who stood facing him saw that he thus breathed his last, he said, "Truly this man was the Son of God" (Mark 15:39).

In his death, Jesus, who had died as a reject, a blasphemer, and political rabble-rouser, now appears for what he really is: the innocent just one who is the victim of the sin of the world, the blind, absolutized, and oppressive social, intellectual, and religious structures of humanity. With his death, the final mask has been removed, and reality is seen for what it really is.

Chapter 6

BEYOND ALL BORDERS

Go into the whole world
[Mark 16:16].

In the past, the God of Israel had shown himself powerful over the nations of the world. He had delivered his people from the pharaoh and had led them to the promised land. But now, in the resurrection of Jesus of Nazareth, there was something radically new. God revealed—beyond his sovereignty over Israel, his sovereignty over all peoples—his sovereignty over the destiny of all humankind.

The New Existence

It is evident from reading the New Testament that at the cross even the followers of Jesus were convinced that he had failed and that all their hopes had come to an end. But the resurrection inaugurated a new movement. The scattered disciples are regrouped and begin a new life in the risen Lord.

The fact that Jesus had died a shameful death seemed the ultimate refutation of his message. By allowing him to die the scandalous death on the cross, God—it seemed—had ratified the nearly universal rejection of Jesus. But then the totally unexpected and undreamed-of took place. The two poles of the early kerygma framed the amazing truth: "You killed him . . . but God raised him from the dead" (Acts 2:23–24, 3:15, 4:10, 6:30). There is no doubt that the resurrection of Jesus was and is at the core of the Christian faith and life: "If Christ has not been raised, our preaching is void of content and your faith is empty too" (1 Cor. 15:14).

From the reading of the gospel accounts, it becomes evident that Jesus did not just return from the dead, as did Lazarus. Jesus died but God raised him to a *new* existence. Upon meeting the risen Lord, even his closest friends did not immediately recognize him. He was the same Jesus, yet there was something different. There was continuity with the preresurrection Jesus, yet there was also a discontinuity. The earthly Jesus had been transformed into the risen Lord. He is with them, but no longer circumscribed by the restrictions of time and space. Mark even says explicitly that he was revealed to them "completely changed in appearance" (16:12). Yet this changed and transformed Jesus is eventually recognized by them as the Jesus of Nazareth whom they had known before—the glorified and risen Lord is Jesus, the crucified.

The gospel accounts of the appearances of Jesus note that the apostles had an experience of Jesus as risen and alive. Throughout the gospels there is a continued emphasis on the dual dimension of the risen Lord: continuity and change. Lane states: "There is an underlying identity within transformation between the historical Jesus and the risen Jesus."[1] This is very difficult for us to understand because we are dealing with a reality that belongs to a new mode of being. It is very real, yet it is beyond the categories of our experience of time and space.

Encounter with the risen Lord transforms those who experience him. Recalling how meeting with certain persons has deeply affected us and might have changed us can help us somewhat to understand what happened in the encounter between the apostles and the risen Lord. But we can never fully understand it: no human encounter can be fully adequate to the encounter with the risen Lord.

This transforming encounter was an illuminating experience as well, for through it the apostles begin to see the entire way of Jesus in a new light— that is, in the light of a deepened faith. Those who had followed Jesus from Galilee with some degree of faith now recognize him in a different way, and in this recognition of him as the risen Lord they are themselves transformed and illuminated. Those who encounter the risen Lord are created anew from within, with the result that they relate in a new way to God, to other persons, institutions, and the world. It is a totally new way of situating themselves within the human condition.

Paul cites as a "proof" of "our status as adopted sons" the experience of God's sending into their hearts "the spirit of his Son which cries out '*Abba*' " (Gal. 4:6). It is through the experience of the risen Lord that they were reborn and knew themselves to be sons and daughters of the one Father. This transforming experience was the beginning of new life—the beginning of the new creation.

It was in the power of the risen Lord that the early community of faith retraced the meaning of the liberating way of Jesus from Nazareth to Jerusalem and interiorized the meaning of his risen presence. This took place in various ways but especially through the ongoing celebration of what had been so characteristic of Jesus: the joy of table-fellowship with all persons, especially the most rejected and marginated of society. They now begin to relate in a new way to their fellow human beings. There is not a new law to this effect, but a new celebration. The life of unlimited love that will refuse to be limited or enslaved by the letter of any law—written laws, customs, or traditions—now begins to be lived by the followers of the resurrected Lord. True life and happiness is loving as God himself loves, which means the rejection of any humanly made obstacles that limit our ability to love.

Christian love means to be perfect as the heavenly Father is perfect: he makes his sun rise on the evil and the good, and sends rain on the just and the unjust (Matt. 5:43–48).

It is from within the perspective of their new existence and new understanding that the followers of Jesus now begin to look back into their memory of the earthly Jesus in attempting to answer the all-important question: who was Jesus of Nazareth? The experience of resurrection is both an original and an originating experience, for it gives rise to the beginning of the process that brings us into the inner knowledge of the whole inner mystery of Christ—from the incarnation to the resurrection and exaltation.

The community of faith was then and is today the starting point of all christological reflection. Because we believe, because we experience him in faith, because we have been transformed through personal encounter with the risen Lord, we seek to articulate our understanding of this person in whom we have been reborn. The existential believing community, historically and culturally situated, is the starting point of Christian reflection. Any other starting point would tend to be mere theory, speculation, or ideology rather than authentic reflection of the intellect seeking a deeper understanding of the faith—not an abstract faith, but the real, living, dynamic, imperfect, and culturally conditioned life of the church.

In the light of the resurrection, the liberative meaning and necessity of the Galilee-Jerusalem struggle begins to emerge. From the final fulfillment, we go back to the starting point so that we too may walk the same way following the salvific way of Jesus. The resurrected Lord himself sends his followers to the starting point: "Go carry the news to my brothers that they are to go to Galilee, where they will see me." (Mt 28:10). Without the resurrection, the Nazareth-to-Jerusalem process would simply perpetuate the cycle of violence and there would seem to be no way out. But without the Nazareth-to-Jerusalem process, the resurrection experience would easily be reduced to a mere "good feeling" with the Lord, which we could even forget.

The cross without the resurrection would be without value and only a curse, but the resurrection without the way of the cross would be a pure utopic dream or illusion. It is only in the whole mystery of Jesus Christ that the mystery of humanity is truly revealed. It is only in the whole mystery of Christ that the necessary process for the liberation of humanity will take place and be celebrated.

The resurrection is the definitive breakthrough of God that penetrates and transcends the human dilemma in which violence only begets greater violence and new forms of violence. We struggle for liberation only to discover ourselves enslaved in new ways. Humanly speaking, there appears to be no way out. In the way of Jesus we discover that violence can only be eliminated through the power of unconditioned and unlimited love.

This love can be found only in unconditional surrender to the love of

God-*Abba*. Only when we experience the absorbing love of God in Jesus—only when we have been grasped by Christ (Phil. 3:12)—can we become lovers in his style. Only when we experience his love can we begin to love as he does (Phil. 2:7–11; John 4). Only then can we begin to move from the violence that we resort to for the sake of self-preservation (of self, institutions, or groups) to the freely accepted violence that we must endure for the life and liberation of others: "There is no greater love than this: to lay down one's life for one's friends" (John 15:13).

The Spirit of the New Creation

When the day of pentecost came it found them gathered in one place. Suddenly. . . there came a noise like a strong, driving wind. . . . Tongues as of fire appeared, which parted and came to rest on each of them. All were filled with the Holy Spirit. They began to express themselves in foreign tongues. . . . Staying in Jerusalem at the time were devout Jews of every nation. . . . They were much confused because each one heard these men speaking his own language. . . . Peter stood up with the Eleven, raised his voice, and addressed them. . . . "Jesus the Nazarene was a man whom God sent to you. . . . He was delivered up. . . . You even made use of pagans to crucify and kill him. God freed him from death's bitter pangs, however, and raised him up again. . . . You must reform and be baptized . . . in the name of Jesus Christ" (Acts 2:1–38).

In his account of the new pentecost—the harvest feast that commemorated the giving of the convenant on Sinai—Luke uses images reminiscent of the first Sinai ("tongues as of fire"; cf. Exod. 19:18). But those present are not given a new *law*, inscribed on *stone;* they are given the *Spirit* who will re-create them *from within.*

The Spirit ushers in the new creation—a people united in their experience of being accepted and loved by God, freed from the enslaving tendencies of "the world." The Spirit-filled person will live in love, joy, peace, tolerance, goodness, generosity, fidelity, simplicity, and self-control (Gal. 5:22–24).

In presenting the history of the early church in Acts, Luke records the history of the power and works of the Holy Spirit. Nor is it presented simply as a piece of history, but in order to give the church of the future a model to live by.

The prophecies of Jeremiah (31:31–34) and Ezekiel (36:25–29) about the new law "within" and the "new person" are now being fulfilled. The new people of God is about to take possession of its promised land, which is all humanity, all ethnic groupings, all nations. No frontiers can deflect this movement. And the way in which the new people will take possession is very important: not by imposition or conquest, but by the gift of the re-creating Spirit, bringing to perfection—not destroying—what is already there.

There will be a new language, truly universal: the language of *agape*. It is the language of selflessness in the service of others, the language of the radical acceptance and love of the other as other. It is a language of the heart, communicating directly with others regardless of human differences.

The Spirit begins the work of transformation with Jesus' apostles. Before, they had been ignorant, difficult to understand, somewhat exclusivist in their thinking, concerned about getting to the power positions, often ready to resort to violence, and quick to run out at moments of difficulty. But now they appear totally different. Peter, who had even denied the Lord, speaks boldly before the crowds and everyone understands him. Peter and the other disciples were probably just as shocked and surprised as the rest of the crowd, for the Galileans, who had not been understood by anyone, are now understood by everyone! But even more than that. Hotheaded Peter does not call for mobilization of the masses against anyone; he invites all to repentance and acceptance of God's forgiveness.

Society's rejects—now reborn of God—begin to invite everyone to the new way that has been shown to them. All are invited, but they must open their hearts to the influence of the Spirit in order to be converted to the new way of life preached and inaugurated by Jesus.

The reality of the message of Jesus became embodied in the members of the primitive church. It was sealed in their hearts and engraved on their minds. It was not arguments but their new way of life that attested to the truth of their radical newness. They had a new vision, a new code of ethics, a new joy, a new fellowship, a new strength, a new self-confidence, and a new courage that totally surpassed anything the world had ever known before. "Humanly speaking," they simply did not make sense, but they had no doubts whatsoever about their new life and new identity. Material possessions would no longer be a divisive factor; they were freely given to the church to be distributed among the needy. They discovered the joy of giving and sharing, and the happiness of being able to be themselves without the need for masks or artificiality. Through the power of the Spirit, they all experienced a new interpersonal communion. And from the very beginning they understood and accepted with certainty the universal dimension of their new life: it was not just for them, but for all the peoples of the world.

It is evident from Acts that the newly converted continued in their previous religio-cultural ways, but they also went beyond them. They came together regularly to pray, study, help one another, and take part in the breaking of the bread (Acts 2:42). They knew that they had discovered something radically new and uniquely beautiful, but, like any great treasure, it would take time for it to be appreciated fully. Their old ways would not be discarded overnight. Their new life did not signal an abrupt end of their Jewish ways, but their Jewish ways were now lived in a new way. Its exclusivity had been broken through, but the long-term results had only begun. Growth in the new life would demand repeated encounters with a kind of dying, but each such experience would lead to new and richer life.

Communion and communication are the social effects of the new creation. Through the Spirit of infinite love, God begins to liberate humankind from the disaster that it has made of itself. As Genesis portrays it, human beings from the very beginning sought to survive and to better their condition through rebellion and material possessions (Gen. 3), at the cost of the blood of their kin (Gen. 4), and quickly set up institutions to protect their own selfish interests against others (Gen. 11). They seem to think that to survive and to better their lot means competition. But this is not God's way.

In Genesis 10, the list of diverse nations and languages is given as a sign of God's creative blessing. The great diversity of peoples is part of God's design and their harmonious unity is God's will. Unity in diversity is part of God's plan. Genesis 11 presents the de facto situation, showing how it has become the opposite of what God wanted. Babylonia, the powerful nation of the world, is attempting to impose upon all the nations a cultural, political, and religious uniformity. It insists that "our way must be the way for all peoples." The result of this idolatrous uniformity—which makes the way of the powerful appear as God's way for all nations—is hostility, opposition, misunderstanding, and wars among the nations of the world. Fellowship is impossible because there is no trust—everyone is out to get the other. This destroys the harmony of diversity presented in Genesis 10. Diversity is now made to appear as a curse. Participation gives way to competition, communion to warfare, and communication to senseless babbling. This divisive, destructive spirit epitomizes the sin of the world.

But now God has redeemed the world through his son. There is now a new principle of unity at work in the world that will not destroy the rich diversity of the nations of the world, but will harmonize it for the betterment of everyone. Thus the pentecost miracle presents the various peoples of the world as clearly maintaining their own individuality, yet all of them understanding the same language. There are no translators and none are needed, for each one understands perfectly in their own native tongue— through the historico-cultural categories of their own space and time. Different languages and customs need not be obstacles to communion and communication.

The New Universalism

Immediately before the ascension, the risen Lord had given his disciples his final instructions: "You will receive power when the Holy Spirit comes upon you; then you are to be my witnesses . . . even to the ends of the earth" (Acts 1:8).

The mandate is very specific. They are to go forth and proclaim with their lives and their words what they have personally experienced. They are the ones who have both seen and heard Jesus—from his baptism to his ascension. The totality of the way of Jesus, which they have taken part in, they are now to live out and transmit "to the ends of the earth." It is not of their own accord or through their own wisdom and power that they will act and speak; the Spirit will come upon them and lead them not only to the geographical ends of the earth, but to all the strata of human life and human society.

The early spread of Christianity, especially in view of the multiple crossings of religious, cultural, and political boundaries—"polarizations"—that it entailed, was nothing less than miraculous. The first disciples were Galileans. As we have already brought out, they were usually viewed as inferior—"ignoramuses, clods"—by their compatriots. Furthermore, some Galileans, especially among the Zealots, were quite exclusivist in their thinking—"no outsiders allowed in!" The rejected, ghetto-minded, "provincial" Galileans are the ones chosen to go out and invite *everyone* to the way of Jesus! How ridiculous it must have seemed to everyone, including the Galileans themselves.

The composition of the first lists of converts to the way of Jesus shows how "successful" God was with the "unlikely" witness of the Galileans: there were Jewish priests (Acts 6:7), Samaritans (8:4-25), Ethiopians (9:26-40), and a Roman centurion (10:1-48). The new way was for everyone; no one was excluded because of race, color, nationality, class, or culture. What mattered was one's openess to belief in Jesus.

The Spirit guided the community to continue what had been so original and meaningful in the earthly life of Jesus: table-fellowship with all. The joyous table-fellowship was an anticipation of the greater joy yet to be expected—the fullness of the kingdom: "I tell you, many will come from east and west and sit at table with Abraham, Isaac, and Jacob in the kingdom of heaven" (Matt. 8:11). It was the celebration of the universal human family begun but not completed. The various members, without ceasing to be who they were, nonetheless saw themselves and others in such a way that they could come together as scribes, tax collectors, priests, Pharisees, Zealots, Romans, Greeks, Samaritans, Ethiopians . . . to share at the common table.

It was not without struggle and pain that the community was able to break with the cultic gods of its members' backgrounds. The first major conflicts were precisely on this point. Would the Gentiles have to submit to a Jewish rite in order to become Christians? Their grappling with the issues allowed them to go beyond the limitations imposed by pre-Christian categories of thought. The Gentiles would become Christians and develop their own forms of Christian practice and ecclesial life. Thus the way of Jesus took root in the Greco-Roman cultural soil and continued to grow.

It was in joy and fellowship that the early church moved beyond Palestine into the world of Hellenism and eventually that of Rome. It was the beginning of the geographical evangelization of the world, and of the various spheres of human existence in all societies. The course traced by the early church started from the world of persons (Galilee), went to the world of religion (Jerusalem), then moved to the world of ideas (Greece), and finally to the world of socio-legal structures (Rome). All levels of society had to be liberated from the god-making process—the absolutizing of "our way" to the exclusion of other ways and of other persons who do not fit neatly into "our way."

Jewish culture made a great contribution to the history of human development in its adherence to monotheism. Its mistake was to absolutize religion, limiting human achievement and development to the knowledge and observance of religious law.

Greek culture made a great contribution to the history of human development by its discovery of *logos*—discourse, reason, relation, proportion. If the ancient Orient had developed the arts, the fables, the stories—of imperation and supplication—it was the Greeks who created the art of persuasion through the reasoning process: the art of logical demonstration. Through the art and science of clear and precise reasoning, they made enormous intellectual progress. Their mistake was to limit and reduce human nature to *pure reason*. Reason became the only norm of humanness. All who did not appear to be of equal rationality, according to their standards of reason, were despised as savages, barbarians. For the Greeks, only a small elite could arrive at the fullness of human personality; the masses were doomed to a subservient existence—manual labor for the sake of the elite.

Finally came the genius of Rome. The Romans were not only the great conquerors of the world, but the great builders of roads and cities, and of the human mechanisms needed to administer a great empire. They were the practical thinkers who could create the necessary bureaucracy to keep an empire functional. They were the founders of the "law and order society." The Roman contribution to world advancement was so great that some even saw in the *pax romana* the ultimate human preparation for the coming of the messianic kingdom of peace and justice. There is no doubt that humanity needs political organization for the assurance of peace and order, but the mistake of the Romans was that they reduced and limited human potential to the political, economic, and military dimensions of human nature. They appreciated Greek thought and tolerated other religions, but it was the state that was all-important. Caesar was God!

Into this world of exclusiveness—Jewish religion, Greek thought, Roman politics—came the church of Jesus of Nazareth with the folly of unlimited love. The Jewish hero had been the person who knew and observed the law with the utmost care; the Greek hero had been the man (not woman!) who could rise above the affairs of the earth to contemplate eternal truth; the Roman hero had been the person who not only conquered others but also ruled over them. Into this world of heroes came a new image of the true hero—the Christian ideal of the martyrs, the saints, who were the foolish lovers who could rise above the interests and intrigues of this world to follow Christ in the way of humility, poverty, obedience to God, faith, hope, and love. It was the new human model that reflects not the long face of the righteous religious fanatic, or the cold, other-worldliness of the detached intellectual, or the tough-killer image of the triumphant emperor, but the happiness of inner joy and tranquility that comes through the experience of being loved by God and loving others. What humanity with all its genius had been seeking—and finding only partially—Jesus of Nazareth brings to the world: the joy and ultimate security that God's love alone can provide.

Christian love will not take persons out of the world—that is, away from concerns for security in ordinary life—but it will lead them to relativize their importance. Food, shelter, and protection are needed for human well-being, but they are not the most important needs. Beyond the most obvious and ordinary needs of human beings there are deeper ones—the need to be accepted, valued, respected, and loved not for what they can accomplish, or because of what groups they belong to, or because of what they look like, or because of how much they possess, but simply because *they are who they are*. As persons begin to respond to the deeper needs of acceptance and love, the way that they respond to such needs as food, shelter, and status will change, for self-preservation will be better seen not as the object of the struggle of one group against another, but as the goal of cooperative effort.

Diverse civilizations had tried to better the human condition in diverse—partial—ways, but Christianity was clear about the great distance between human expectations and the capacity of human methods to achieve them. The best of human ways always tended to be exclusive, partial; the way of Jesus incorporated all the others, functioned through all of them, and went beyond them. Christianity did not eliminate the need for seeking human solutions to human problems, but it pointed out that no human solution would be the total answer to the problems confronting humankind.

Emperor Julian, in a letter to the high priest Arsace, expressed his astonishment that a "universal philanthropy," unknown until then, should be the ordinary way of life of uncouth Galileans. What the world had never thought of or attempted, some unlettered Galileans had introduced: belief in the universal equality and fellowship of all human beings as adopted sons and daughters of the one God.

In terms of security, the Jews had contributed to posterity the security of religion, the Greeks had contributed the security of rational knowledge, and the Romans had contributed the security of law and order. But it was Galileans who contributed the ultimate security: that of being loved simply for being oneself and the capacity to love others in the same way.

Jesus had affirmed Jewishness by being and living as a Jew, but he rebuked it for its religious enslavement. Paul became "like a Gentile" (1 Cor. 9:19–23) but, from within the Greek world, he condemned the limitations and "foolishness" of Greek wisdom (1 Cor. 1). Christianity, as it spread to other parts of the world, sought to take up what was good in, and bring ultimate liberation to, all the strata of human life—the personal, religious, intellectual, social.

The way of Jesus is not simply *another* alternative among the countless others that humankind has devised and will devise in time to come. It is *the* alternative. It is radically different from all merely human ways of life or problem-solving schemes. It comes "in the manner of" human nature (incarnation/continuity) but it differs from it by transcending it (resurrection/discontinuity).

As in the risen Lord, so too in the person and life of the Christian there is continuity and discontinuity: I am the person I was before, but now I situate myself differently in the life that I live in the same world. From within the new perspective of the Spirit, I am led to review and interrogate and relativize all human ways, institutions, values, and religious practices. This new way of relating with self, others, society, the world, and God allows one to die to the enslaving absolutes of the world and live a liberated and liberating existence amid its multiple enslavements.

The way of Jesus, continued by the Spirit now present in us, begins in the human heart, liberating us from the enslavement of egotism. It penetrates to the deepest level of human society, liberating peoples from false or only partially true images of God. It penetrates the various systems of human knowledge and science, liberating them from their intrinsic limitations. It penetrates the social institutions of humankind, liberating them from their inner tendency to enslave the very persons they were meant to serve.

The foundational relationship between Christian faith and the cultural milieu is of the very essence of the way of Jesus. It is founded on the historical genesis of the church as it moved from Galilee to Rome, and it is fundamental to the dynamism of the gospel today as it seeks to convert human hearts, and thus the whole of creation.

PART THREE

From Margination to New Creation

The historico-cultural situation of Galilee, Jerusalem, Greece, and Rome are constitutive elements of the life, work, and message of Jesus and the apostolic church. It is upon the full reality of the embryonic church that subsequent theological reflection must seek to base itself. The more we can appreciate the concrete situation of Jesus and the early church, the more we can appreciate the concrete aspects of the divine plan for humankind, then and now. Because the way of Jesus and the early church are the original and originative experience of Christianity, they become the normative memory and the normative criterion of the Christian church for all ages.

As we study the way of Jesus, we discover three basic principles that will guide us in interpreting and rejuvenating human reality today in terms of the gospel: the Galilee principle, the Jerusalem principle, and the resurrection principle.

In this final part of our work we will bring out how in the person of Jesus of Nazareth the full meaning of the Mexican-American struggle for identity, integration, and celebration of new life becomes luminous. Our situation and struggles were anticipated by him, and in his situation and struggles the meaning and purpose of our own come to light. Today Jesus continues his struggle for new life in our struggles, and it is in him and through him that we discover the ultimate purpose and goal of our struggles.

We have done a cultural rereading of the gospels; now it is time to do a gospel rereading of our cultural life.

Chapter 7

THE GALILEE PRINCIPLE

*God chose those whom the world
considers absurd [1 Cor. 1:28].*

The first principle for the New Testament interpretation of the contemporary situation is the Galilee principle: *what human beings reject, God chooses as his very own.*

For Mexican-American Christians, it is in the light of the gift of faith that they discover their ultimate identity as God's chosen people. It is in the cultural identity of Jesus the Galilean that the ultimate meaning of their cultural identity becomes clear.

Their *mestizaje* is their Galilean identity and challenge. The world's rejection of *mestizaje* is not unrelated to God's choice of it. What the world rejects, God chooses—to advance the historical working out of the *eschaton*, the final age, one step further. With each new *mestizaje*, some racio-cultural frontiers that divide humankind are razed and a new unity is formed.

The Way of Jesus

That Jesus was the Son of God become man is at the very core of the Christian creed and the history of humanity. We can hardly improve on St. Paul's magnificent expression of astonishment and wonder at this central implication of the incarnation:

> Though he was in the form of God,
> he did not deem equality with God
> something to be grasped at.
> Rather, he emptied himself
> and took the form of a slave,
> being born in human likeness [Phil. 2:6–7].

Or, as Juan Mateos translates the text in the *Nueva Biblia Española*, "as one among so many." He became a human being without any particular privilege or status. Even more, he assumed the form of a *slave*: an inferior human according to the standards of the dominant segment of an unbalanced society.

The Epistle to the Hebrews sheds some light on the reason for this abasement. The new priesthood inaugurated by Jesus does not offer sacrifices—other persons or things victimized—for the suffering of the world. He sacrificed not others but himself for the sake of the world.

The new priesthood heals suffering by assuming the sickness, the weakness, the infamy of a moribund world. Jesus becomes weak in order that we might become strong; he dies in order that we might live.

Jesus can have compassion on the weak and erring because he himself has lived through the same situation. Without ceasing to be God, he entered the world of the voiceless, the sick, the hungry, the oppressed, the public sinners, the emarginated, the suffering. He did not come just to *do* certain things *for* them: he came to *become* one of them, so as to enable *them* to find new life in him and thus be able to do things for themselves.

He was one of the millions of rejected persons in the history of humankind, but he was not "just another" reject. He not only rejected rejection, but enables his followers to do likewise. He did not gather unto himself the suffering of the world in order to canonize and legitimate suffering, but to transform it into the creative force for a new creation.

What is stated so succinctly in Philippians and Hebrews is brought out concretely and graphically by Jesus' entire Galilean ministry. God could have started anywhere, but de facto he became a Galilean Jew and Galilee was the starting point of his mission.

I contend that the Galilean identity is the essential starting point of Christian identity and mission today—and everyday, until the final coming of Christ. Marginality as symbolized by Galilee is one of the key functional concepts of the inner dynamism of the gospel.

We have to be aware of what Galilee was and what it meant to be a Galilean so as to discover the places and peoples with a similar identity and role in today's world. It was said that nothing good could come out of Galilee. God ignored them and chose it as his starting point. He revealed himself in what the world ignored. It is there that the unsuspected event took place. It is in the unsuspected places and situations of the world and through "unlikely" persons that God continues to work today.

The Church's Witness to Poverty

In trying to follow the footsteps of the Master, the church has always freely chosen poverty as an indispensable requisite. How we have understood and lived out this poverty can certainly be questioned, but that poverty is of the essence of the imitation of Christ cannot be doubted.

"Blessed are you poor" (Luke 6:20). They are God's chosen ones. Jesus becomes one of them and demands of his disciples that they relinquish their worldly possessions and follow him. He warns them against ambitions of power and prestige. Priority is to be given to the ones in greatest need. If we are to follow him, we are to freely separate ourselves from whatever separates us from the needy of the world so that we might enter into solidarity with them. To do something for them is to do it for God. The way they are treated, God is treated. Where they are, God is.

It should not be at all surprising that among the Christian heroes most universally venerated by believers is Francis of Assisi, who chose radical poverty for the sake of the kingdom of God. He certainly could have been rich, but freely chose to be poor—not for the sake of poverty itself, but in order to serve the poor. In Latin America, Saint Martin de Porres, who devoted his life to working among the poorest of the poor, is probably the most venerated saint today. He was widely acclaimed by the people even before his official canonization. For her work and witness in India, Mother Teresa has captivated the minds and hearts of a world enslaved by materialism and greed. The canonical religious life has always been looked upon as a more intense way of following the way of Jesus, and poverty has always been one of its essential, constitutive vows. To be a religious is to freely and joyfully choose poverty and to dedicate one's life to the service of the poor.

It is to the poor that the church commits itself and not to the state of poverty as such—as if it were promoting indigence for its own sake. The poor are the blessed and chosen of God because the sinful world has condemned them to poverty. The mechanisms of the wealthy that cause the extreme poverty of the masses were clearly condemned as antievangelical by the Latin American bishops at Puebla (no. 1159).

The poor will not be liberated from their misery by becoming wealthy but by discovering a new image of humanity that is now possible in Jesus. The religious freely chooses the scandal of poverty so as to enter into solidarity with the victims of injustice. This witness of the church is very powerful; it challenges the social norms of "acceptability" based on wealth, power, and prestige. It tells the poor that they, even though deprived by the world, are beautiful, desirable, and worthy of respect. It is the most powerful proclamation of the gospel—to proclaim the fundamental dignity of the undignified of the world, and not by words only but by freely and joyfully choosing to live among them and share their lot in life, not as strangers or distant "do-gooders," but truly as one of them.

Poverty that results from injustice and exploitation is the most visible and striking sign of the sin of the world. Like Jesus, the members of religious orders assume this condition so as to liberate the oppressed from the multiple bondage to which they have been subjected by the structures of the powerful.

If the church is to be a faithful witness of the Master, it must be identified with the poor and the oppressed of the world. If instead it is identified with the rich, the installed, and the powerful, it betrays by its life the very gospel it proclaims in words. Poverty, in solidarity with the poor, is of the essence of church life. A church that is not poor will not be the light of Christ in the midst of the darkness of today's world.

The third general conference of Latin American bishops, meeting at Puebla, Mexico, in 1979, following the inspiration of Pope John Paul II, did not hesitate to state the preferential though not exclusive concern of the church for the poor and oppressed of the world:

> When we draw near to the poor in order to accompany them and serve them, we are doing what Christ taught us to do when he became our brother, poor like us. Hence service to the poor is the privileged, though not exclusive, gauge of our following of Christ [no. 1145].
>
> Commitment to the poor and oppressed and the rise of grassroots communities have helped the church to discover the evangelizing potential of the poor. For the poor challenge the church constantly, summoning it to conversion; and many of the poor incarnate in their lives the evangelical values of solidarity, service, simplicity, and openness to accepting the gift of God [no. 1147].

And quoting directly from John Paul II's address at the *barrio* of Santa Cecilia (January 30, 1979) they went on to state:

> This central feature of evangelization was stressed by Pope John Paul II: "I have earnestly desired this meeting because I feel solidarity with you, and because you, being poor, have a right to my special concern and attention. I will tell you the reason: the pope loves you because you are God's favorites. In founding his family, the church, God had in mind poor and needy humanity. To redeem it, he sent his Son specifically, who was born poor and lived among the poor to make us rich with his poverty (2 Cor. 8:9)" [no. 1143].

Even though the church has not always lived out this ideal, and even though the exact meaning and implications have certainly been doubted and questioned, the ideal itself has never been questioned. The gospel of the Son of God who freely became poor for our salvation has always been the fundamental constitution of the church. Throughout the entire scripture message, the poor are the privileged of God. God lives with them and among them. It is in the face and person of Jesus the poor Galilean that the face of God is manifested.

From Rejection to Election

Sinful humanity has been very creative in figuring out ways to reject and dehumanize persons and entire peoples. It seems easy for many to accept the idea that God is the creator of all—but not *live out* belief that God created each and every person to his own image and likeness.

There are multiple counts on which persons and peoples are rejected and set apart as undesirable: race, color, class, language, nationality, size, age, shape, hair, status, personality, schooling, dress, religion, politics, family name, neighborhood, behavior, friends. . . . God made us to be a family, but we seem determined to tear each other apart. We form fraternities and clubs so as to be together with our own—only to rip each other apart with jealousies and intrigues. We want to have a sense of belonging and acceptance, but live in constant fear of rejection and aloneness.

The poor are commonly understood to be those who lack material possessions, those who have less than they need, those who are of lesser worth, who arouse pity, who are inferior in quality or value, and finally those who are unproductive. We might add: those who have lost the desire to live because their lives no longer seem worth living.

For our purposes, we may distinguish three basic types of poverty: material, psychological, and cultural-spiritual. *Material* poverty is the lack of the fundamental necessities of life, such as food, clothing, housing, and medicine. It means not having money or credit. It means not having a job or even the possibility of one. It means being broke.

In many ways, material poverty is the basis of the other kinds of poverty, because those who control the material things of society also control the institutions that regulate every aspect of life. They determine the criteria of acceptability by which all others will be judged worthy or unworthy, acceptable or unacceptable, superior or inferior.

Everyone has basic psychological needs, and when these are not met there is *psychological* poverty. Everyone needs to be accepted, esteemed, needed, understood, desired, and loved. If these needs are not met, persons develop a low self-image and will often fear or even hate themselves. One of the great problems in the world is that because of psychological poverty many persons do not love or accept themselves as they are. Because of the standards or norms projected by those in control, some persons see themselves as ugly, inferior, or without dignity. They see themselves as unwanted and undesirable.

A person could be materially rich while being psychologically poor, and vice versa. But most materially poor persons also experience psychological poverty insofar as they experience themselves to have less than the wealthy who determine what it means to be "successful." The poor cannot afford all the beauty treatments, proper diets, exercise, clothing, and various gadgets to make themselves appear "beautiful and desirable" to themselves and to society. They cannot afford the dental work to straighten their teeth, the sculptured haircuts to give them that carefully executed "natural look," the tailored clothing to make them appear as competent business executives by daytime and sexy lovers by night. They cannot afford the proper schools to enable them to speak "correctly," nor can they enter the "right" fraternities that would give them the "right" connections in life. They cannot go to exclusive clubs or stay at expensive hotels.

All these factors and many more combine to give many persons a poor image of themselves, while the wealthy develop an exaggerated image of their superiority. Persons become conscious that they belong to different groups and that they cannot break from one group into another. No matter how morally good the poor might be, there is a deep consciousness that they belong to a lesser class, and no matter how morally bad the rich might be, they are convinced they belong to a higher class. Within one's own class, one might have a high image of oneself and be quite secure, yet in relation to persons of a higher socio-economic class, one knows and experiences inferiority and distance. The consciousness of class difference is very profound. Even when persons from the lower classes become quite rich, they are looked upon as *"nouveau riche"*; they do not really belong to the "elite." Class consciousness is so strong and persistent that it is like a permanent identity mark on the soul of the person.

The third and deepest level of poverty is cultural-spiritual poverty. Cultural and spiritual are not exactly the same, but they are intimately interrelated, for basic culture is in many ways the fundamental life-spirit of the group. Cultural-spiritual poverty is the deprivation not only of goods or status, but of the very humanity of a racially and culturally determined group.

When a group is labeled "culturally deprived," it has been robbed of its humanity by the group that does the labeling. The group in power will project its own image of itself—its color, its physique, its psychology, its culture, its foods, its language, its accent, its humor, its clothing, its religion—as the only one that is authentically human. Although the less wealthy within the power group will have a sense of belonging to a lower class, they still consider themselves *human* and members of the same race. Nevertheless even the wealthiest and best educated of an oppressed racio-cultural group—who might be even richer and better educated than those at the very top of the power group—will be looked upon as inferior human beings because they are of an "inferior" race or culture. They are not just of a lower class, they are of a lesser humanity.

This is the worst type of poverty because it deprives persons of their fundamental humanity as shaped and determined by the Creator. Persons are conditioned to see beauty, acceptability, and respectability only in the ways of the power group and often feel ashamed or at least confused about their own characteristics. Some even curse their own people and their God for making them to be what they are.

Their fundamental spirit is ridiculed, stepped on, and crushed. Their world order no longer has meaning or cohesiveness, because it is questioned and threatened by a *more powerful* world order, which imposes itself as *superior.* Their own people and well intentioned outsiders try to help them "improve" by ceasing to be who they are—forgetting their language, dress, customs, and religion—so as to become "better"—which means "like the dominant group." Within the group some might be affluent and have a healthy self-image, but in relation to the power group they will usually have a deep feeling of resentment and inferiority. Even the worst of the power group will appear to them to be superior. Such a view of one's group tends to damage seriously or even totally destroy the innermost spirit of a group.

Sometimes members of "superior" groups wonder why conquered or defeated groups appear to be lifeless and without motivation. It is too easily assumed that they *gave up* something, when in fact it was *taken from* them. Another group deeply wounded them and tried to destroy the life-giving spirit given to them by the Creator who molded them out of their own particular earth, gave them the pigment of their skin and the shape of their bones, the color of their eyes and the texture of their hair, their language and their way of life—"and God saw that it was good."

When the group in power in a multiethnic society is of a different color, culture, language, and religion, and it imposes the image of itself as the only one legitimately human, beautiful, and dignified, then only this image is reflected in sacred objects and rites. Such an imposition robs the poor of the God-image after which they were made and which they reflect in their lives.

I contend that this is the worst type of poverty and oppression, because it so interiorizes the image of the oppressor as superior and exclusively Godlike that the oppressed begin to hate themselves *for what they are* and admire the image of the oppressor even in the images of the divine. Even if the oppressed become materially wealthy, they will remain spiritually poor because the powerful have robbed them of the greatest treasure they possess—the God-given spirit that sustains them in their collective life.

Because of this cultural-spiritual poverty, some of a minority group will become ashamed of who they are—in particular the young, who do not want to be labeled backward or primitive. They can struggle to become well educated, wealthy, and powerful, but they cannot change their fundamental earthly or cultural identity: they continue to have the same skin pigmentation, hair, eyes, physique, and collective soul. Because I am not just a member of a group—such as a club, association, or church—but precisely because my people lives in me, because I am bone of their bones and flesh of their flesh, because I am mind of their mind and heart of their heart, I cannot just quit my racio-cultural group. No matter how hard I try, the group is in me and I am in the group—we live in each other. I may succeed in improving myself and become very successful, even according to the standards of the powerful, but I cannot quit myself. I can adapt, improve, degenerate; succeed or fail; but regardless of what I do with myself—good or bad—I am myself to the end.

When this native spirit—the core identity of a group—is crushed, oppressed, stepped upon, ridiculed, exploited, scoffed at as backward, pagan, or superstitious, destroyed through the education of its children in the worldview of an oppressor, taken care of by the social welfare structures of the powerful, and "evangelized" by the churches of the dominant, the oppressed group will be deprived of the deepest necessity of human beings: fundamental earthly belonging.

Even though many members of a people that is culturally deprived of its native spirit will give in under the tremendous burden and live a lifeless existence, there will always be some—a faithful remnant—who will refuse to give in, who will refuse to die. In spite of all the insults and opposition, they will continue proudly to be who they are.

It is a great tribute to the Jewish people that in spite of the great suffering and constant humiliation throughout their history, they remained a people because of their deep faith in God and their uncompromising pride in being a distinctive people. This does not mean that they were perfect or without sin. But it does bring out the fact that spiritual strength is the most powerful force in the survival of a people. Within their ranks, there were certainly rich and poor, powerful and powerless. Yet as a people they were strong in the absolute conviction of the Spirit—the God of Abraham and of Isaac, of Jacob and of Moses—who sustained them in existence and would liberate them from their oppressors. This was the source of their strength and the guarantee of their survival. Yet, as extrabiblical sources bring out, the cultural expressions of their native spirit were certainly threatened by the lifestyles of Greece and Rome.

The Jewish people of Galilee experienced all three types of poverty. They were the simple and hardworking people of the land. Because of the great fertility of the land, they did not live in extreme poverty, but they certainly do not appear to have been wealthy. In a Latin American light, we might describe them as hardworking *"campesinos."* They were considered psychologically and sociologically inferior even by their own people, and they were considered culturally inferior by the great powers of the world. They were materially, psychologically, sociologically, and culturally poor. As a whole, they were stubborn, backward Jews to the Romans and the Greeks, and impure, *mestizo* "country bumpkins" to their fellow Jews. By any of the common standards of acceptability, they were "inferior."

In the quest for identity and belonging, the *mestizo*'s double cultural margination functions in a way similar to that of the Galileans, who were the "little people" of the land at the time of Jesus.

The cultural parent groups of the *mestizo* normally tend to reject their cultural child and its cultural identity because it does not appear to be the perfect mirror of their own identity. The *mestizo* is partly their own, but it is partly other and foreign. As a *mestizo* you are allowed to live, but you are not allowed to have a life of your own. You will always appear deficient by the norms of both parent groups and therefore never fully acceptable to either. Yet the parent cultures are not destroyed in the *mestizo,* but mutually combined so as to form a new entity. The great tragedy of *mestizo* existence is that the parent cultures do not see their child in a loving way, but rather tend to look upon it as a mixture of "good and bad," a misfit, a nonequal.

If cultural-spiritual poverty is the worst type of oppression, *mestizaje* is the worst type of human rejection because it brings with it a *double* alienation and margination. The *mestizo* is not allowed to feel at home anywhere.

The pain of rejection is made much worse when not only the structures of society reject you, but even the structures of religion participate actively in the rejection. The "little people" who believe in Christ have not, for the most part, been welcomed in official church buildings and celebrations, which are supposed to be actualizations of Christ's presence. It was not infrequent for Mexican-Americans to hear from the lips of an ordained priest: "This is not your church . . . get out of here!" "Respectable" Catholics did not want to worship alongside those "smelly Mexicans"; practical-minded "Christians" did not want those unruly Hispanics around messing things up. Church was, and in many places continues to be, for the "nice ones" who can afford to dress up and behave according to the accepted norms of the established society. For the others, there was and often continues to be a very unambiguous message: "You are not wanted here . . . you do not belong here."

The "little ones" of society have been treated by the churches of today as the Galileans were treated by the "temple clique" of Jerusalem. The Jerusalemites would have liked for them to stay out; they were undesirables. The word of the Son of man, judging all the nations of the world, was fulfilled in them: "I was a stranger (according to human standards, I was not an acceptable member of your group) and you did not welcome me (you did not make me feel as one of your own)" (Matt. 25:43).

Where "rejects" are exiled from the official churches, Christ is likewise expelled with them. Generally speaking, church leaders have not gone out searching for "undesirables"; worse yet, some are still chasing them away for what appear to them to be good liturgical or canonical reasons. The parable of the straying sheep in Matthew 18:10–14 has, generally speaking, not been understood to apply to the unwanted of society. But Jesus, the beloved son of the Father who does not want a single one of his own to be lost, defends these "little ones" tenaciously, just as a mother protects all but especially the smallest of her children. Jesus stays with them; he stays again in "Galilee."

Out of this suffering of rejection should logically come an attitude of fatalism, hatred, resentment, anger, and vengeance. Yet in their Christian faith a *mestizo* people can see another alternative, which alone can break the hellish cycle of violence: because their suffering has been intense, even more intense must be their desire to initiate something new so that others will not have to suffer what they have had to suffer. It is the translation of this desire into practice that ushers in the new creation, the process of liberation for everyone.

Galilean Identity Today

Because *mestizo* groups have suffered at the deepest level of human existence, they can be compassionate with the suffering of others. The unshaka-
ble knowledge that the one who saves is indeed alive and working through
them urges them to celebrate and proclaim what they believe:

> The Spirit of God is upon me; he has anointed me to preach the gospel
> to the poor. He has sent me to proclaim release to the captives . . . and
> to set at liberty those who are oppressed. . . . Today this scripture has
> been fulfilled in your ears [Luke 4:18–21].

Because they know the pain of rejection, they also experience the burning
need for that core human liberation that comes only through acceptance,
belonging, love, and generosity. Their being deprived of love as a group but
having experienced it in their intimate family circles has intensified their
need and desire for love beyond the range of family and immediate group.

In the light of the liberating life and message of Jesus we see the condition
of double rejection as a sign of divine election: because a group's suffering
and rejection has been great, equally great is its capacity for loving. What it
has been deprived of, it must make possible for all. Mexican-Americans
have experienced acceptance within their families; now, with *Papacito Dios*
and *la Virgen María,* they must share it with the society that has refused it to
them—this is the Christian pedagogy of the oppressed.

For those who ordinarily have a good existential sense of belonging, the
idea of being chosen is nothing special. But for one who has been consistently ignored or rejected, the fact of being noticed, accepted, and chosen is
not only good news, but new life. For in being chosen, what was nothing
becomes something; what was dead now comes to life. In the light of the
Judeo-Christian tradition, the Mexican-American experience of rejection
and margination is converted from human curse to the very sign of divine
predilection. It is evident from the scriptures that God chooses the outcasts
of the world—not exclusively, but certainly in a preferential way. Those
whom the world ignores, God goes out of his way to love with a special
love. Nor does he choose the poor and the lowly just to keep them down
and make them feel good in their misery. Such an election would be the
very opposite of good news; it would truly make of Christianity the
opium to keep the poor quiet and domesticated. God chooses the
poor and the marginated of the world to be the agents of the new creation.

The experience of being wanted *as one is*, of being needed and of being
chosen, is a real and profound rebirth. Those who had been made to consider themselves inferior, will now begin to appreciate what it feels like to be
accepted fully as human beings. Out of their new self-image, new powers
will be released that had always been there but had not been able to surface.

Through this experience, the sufferings of the past are healed though not forgotten—and they should not be forgotten, for it is precisely out of the condition of suffering that the poor are chosen to initiate a new way of life where others will not have to suffer what the poor suffered in the past. When one forgets the experience of suffering, as has happened to many immigrant groups in the U.S.A.—such as the Irish in Boston—then they simply inflict the same insults and worse upon others that had previously been inflicted upon them. The greater the suffering and the more vivid the memory of it, the greater the challenge will be to initiate changes so as to eliminate the root causes of the evils that cause suffering. It is the wounded healer who has not forgotten the pain of the wounds who can be the greatest healer of the illnesses of society.

It is in their margination from the centers of the various establishments that Mexican-Americans live the Galilean identity today. Because they are inside-outsiders, they appreciate more clearly the best of the traditions of both groups, while also appreciating the worst of the situation of both. It is precisely in this double identity that they have something of unique value to offer both. The very reasons for their margination are the bases of their liberating and salvific potential not only for themselves but for others as well.

It is consistently in the frontier regions of human belonging that God begins the new creation. Established centers seek stability; frontier regions can risk to be pioneers. It is "frontier types" who will be the trailblazers of new societies:

> The stone which the builders rejected has become the keystone of the structure. It is the Lord who did this and we find it marvelous to behold [Matt. 21:42].

As *mestizos* of the borderland between Anglo America and Latin America, Mexican-Americans can be instrumental in bringing greater appreciation and unity between the peoples of the two Americas. Both have much to offer to each other but as long as they are separated by destructive stereotypes of each other and the quest for power or vengeance, they will never be able to come together for the betterment of both.

One of the great problems between the two Americas is the lack of understanding and communication. They are two totally different worlds. Each one has its own values, meanings, and symbols. It is not a question of which is better or which is worse. Both are rich in many ways and poor in many ways. The Mexican-American stands in the midst of both worlds and what in effect appears as an unfinished identity can be the basis for personal understanding and appreciation of two identities. It is through the Mexican-American that the two Americas will meet, know, and love each other.

If Latin America has always celebrated *el día de la raza* as the beginning of the new race made up of Latin Europeans and native Americans, so today the Mexican-American can celebrate the beginning of a *nueva raza* that is beginning to bring together Latin America and Anglo America. Two great historico-cultural traditions are meeting and fusing into a new historico-cultural tradition in the person of the Mexican-American. Even though the Mexican-Americans have been despised by both parent cultures, nevertheless it is they who have been culturally prepared to be, in God's grace, the liberators of and the bearers of peace to both parent groups. God has chosen them to be his historical agents of a new unity—not a new North American conquest, but truly a new creation.

The joyful message of liberation is being celebrated and proclaimed loudly and clearly in the hearts, homes, streets, *barrios,* and churches where Mexican-American Christians continue to celebrate their Christian experience as interiorized in them through the power of the Spirit. Where the church has not deserted a people, the people has not deserted the church. Yet even where the institutional church has deserted or ignored the Mexican-American community, they have faithfully continued to practice and celebrate their ecclesial faith in their own way and in their own homes.

Within the institutions themselves there are those who are beginning to discover that Christ is truly present among the "nobodies" of society, announcing that the kingdom of God is at hand. Among them, in their *posadas, pastorelas, devociones, rosarios,* and other celebrations, he is loudly proclaiming that liberation and peace is at hand—the liberation and peace which although not of this world is nevertheless inaugurated in this world. None of the suffering poor should fail to understand and make their own the word of Christ: ". . . look up and raise your heads, because your liberation is at hand" (Luke 21:28). It is in Christ that the heads of the rejected can truly be raised high with the pride that it is in and through them that the expected liberation and peace of the world is now beginning.

Westminster United Presbyterian Church
1501 WEST CLEVELAND RD.
SOUTH BEND, INDIANA 46628

Chapter 8

THE JERUSALEM PRINCIPLE

> *As the time approached when he*
> *was to be taken from the world,*
> *he firmly resolved to proceed*
> *toward Jerusalem [John 15:16].*

It is in the Galilean identity of Jesus that the ultimate meaning of the cultural identity of an oppressed people is to be sought. It finds expression in what we have called the Galilee principle—namely, what human beings reject, God chooses as his very own.

Similarly, it is in Jesus' way from Galilee to Jerusalem, and the culmination of his salvific public ministry there, that the ultimate meaning of an oppressed people's *mission to society* is to be sought. It finds expression in what we call the Jerusalem principle: God chooses an oppressed people, not to bring them comfort in their oppression, but to enable them to confront, transcend, and transform whatever in the oppressor society diminishes and destroys the fundamental dignity of human nature.

No matter how powerful or successful a people or society may be, it must ultimately be judged in the light of God's truth, the operative word of the gospels. No matter how useful, powerful, or sacred a person, institution, or site may be, it must be confronted with the word of truth in the service of love.

This is not an easy confrontation. In our ordinary way of doing things, we find it easy to confront the strong and the powerful because we would love to be where they are, have what they have. But such a confrontation is not evangelical. It liberates no one; if "successful," it merely puts new faces in old slots and does not really change anything. This is the problem with so many human revolutions: the top changes, the middle is adjusted a little, but the base of the socio-political pyramid usually stays the same or is even worse off than before. Even Jesus' *mode* of confrontation is radically different from the ways of the world. But it is the only one that introduces the radical change that human nature needs but is incapable of by itself.

103

Our Way to Jerusalem

If the liberating way of Jesus had stopped in Galilee, we would be forced to agree with the critics of Christianity who claim that religion is but the opium of the masses. But Jesus did not stop there. He made it known in no uncertain terms that he *had* to go to Jerusalem. The New Testament uses a very graphic expression; it says that he "hardened his face to go to Jerusalem" (Luke 9:51). The confrontation with the power structures in Jerusalem would certainly mean suffering and death, yet it had to be undertaken; there was no other way.

In our times, and in all times, Christ has to go his way to Jerusalem. Again he has to face the structures of oppression in today's world. As his Galilean followers were called to go with him, so today his followers are likewise called to go with him and in him to the Jerusalems of today's world. God chooses disciples not just to make them feel good, but for a mission. "I have chosen you to go out and bear much fruit" (John 15:16). To accept God's election is not a passive privilege, but an active mission. It is a call to be prophetic in both deeds and words. It is a call to live a new alternative in the world and to invite others to this new way.

Fidelity to Christ means to stay with him on his way to Jerusalem; to depart from that way would be infidelity. The followers of Jesus are called to remain in this world, but not to be of this world. Conformity to the ways of the world would be a betrayal to the way of Christ, which is that of confrontation with the ways of the world.

In fidelity to his way, Mexican-American Christians are challenging the oppressive powers of today, both within the Latin American world and in the U.S.A. They do not want to inflict violence on others, but they know they have the mission to make known in no uncertain terms the injustice and violence that the establishments are inflicting on the "little people" on the fringes of human belonging, or outside it altogether.

They do not want to inflict suffering on others, but neither do they want others to have to suffer what they have been forced to suffer. Their intention is not simply to turn things upside down so that they will end up doing unto others what others had been doing unto them. This is not the revolution that Mexican-Americans should be searching for; it would amount to keeping the vicious cycle of violence spinning. They do not want simply to join the structures, or even to take them over; they want to liberate oppressive structures and all those who are enslaved by them.

We do not go to "Jerusalem" to burn or to kill. With Christ we cry out in compassion for the oppressing and blind establishment, which is itself enslaved and decaying: "O Jerusalem, Jerusalem, you killed the prophets and stoned those who are sent to you . . . would that even today you knew the things that make for peace" (Luke 13:34; 19:42). Christ, the Son, was not sent into the world to condemn it, but that it might be saved through him (John 3:17). In the most touching terms Jesus makes clear that he willed their life, their liberation, their peace: "How often would I have gathered your children together as a hen gathers her brood under her wings . . . but you would not" (Luke 13:34).

Martin Luther King, Jr., also dreamed of the liberation of his people and of racists alike. He knew that the racists themselves were the victims of their own enslaving structures. They too needed liberation. Mexican-American Christians have well understood the essential nonviolence of the core of Martin Luther King's civil rights movement: the liberation of *all* the enslaved . . . a change of heart for everyone. With Christ and in Christ they do not want to take lives, but rather to give their own—precisely for the liberation of all.

It is important for the "little ones" of society to become conscious that, precisely because of their nothingness, God chooses them for a mission (see 1 Cor. 1). From within their position of powerlessness, they are to come forth and challenge the unjust and enslaving ways of the establishment. God uses the powerlessness of this world to confront and convert the powerful.

Those in power are themselves powerless to bring about their own liberation. The power of the world corrupts and—worse yet—blinds those within the power system to the corruptive force of their own power. They are not aware that they are enslaved and hence they seek only maintenance of the status quo, not liberation. Only powerlessness can liberate abusive power.

Those who have not had false gods to trust in will be freer to recognize the absolutes of the system as false gods. They who are aware of their poverty can better recognize that it is the life-giving Father who alone gives true life. The mission of those on the outskirts of the established order is to *go to the centers* of power and unveil the root causes of the evil that has become engrained in the structures that shape socio-national life and hide the face of the true God who is Father-*Abba* of all.

Jesus said that "the poor will always be with you" (Matt. 26:11; Mark 14:7; John 13:29). We can understand this in a *conditional* sense: as long as there will be absolutized structures that cause enslavement, the poor will be there to confront them. The poor are not simply an "annoyance," or a "necessary evil"; they are the agents of the presence of God's liberative grace. It is through them that God institutes the new creation.

The Church: Beginning of the New Mestizo Creation

The ongoing history of Christianity brings out how the church, from its earliest beginnings, has identified with the structures, values, language, culture, and religion of the place where it was taking root, but at the same time it has differentiated itself from them in various ways. Sometimes, to its own detriment, it has overidentified and confused itself with the cultural structures of its locale.

It is of great interest to us today, when the entire Third World rises in prominence at this moment of history, that the early Christians were identified by the pagan establishment of the second and third centuries precisely as the "third world" or the "third race."[1]

This designation clearly points out that the Christians, like *la raza mestiza* of today, could not be classified according to the classification categories of either the pagans or the Jews. They were both and yet they were neither the one nor the other alone. They were the same and yet they lived differently. They were bound together by a new intimacy and mutual concern that went beyond normal, acceptable behavior within the empire. They lived in the world, but developed a new way of understanding and appreciating persons, the world, and religion. They did not disdain knowledge of the world, but they were developing and pursuing a new knowledge that the world had not discovered. New linguistic expressions were coming forth, new rites were being developed, and new symbols were emerging that confused the learned and the installed of the time. The cross, the world's symbol of curse, was emerging as a privileged symbol of divine blessing.

This new "third race" was turning the world inside out. It made no sense, yet the rich and the poor, the powerful and the powerless, the educated and the uneducated, were converting to it. This new "third race" was in many ways part of them, but it likewise offered them something radically new and it offered society new possibilities.

By being *in* the world but not *of* the world the church by its very nature came to be marginated—an in/out-group. As the conciliar fathers of Vatican II discovered, it cannot be defined clearly and exhaustively by the categories of human language. It can be described, but it cannot be reduced to precise definition. If the church separated itself totally from the world or if it totally identified itself with the world, it would not be of true service to humanity. There have been cases of both extremes throughout the history of the church. Diverse factions want the church to be either the one or the other, but they are threatened by a church that is truly a third entity.

It was difficult for the authorities to classify or identify the church according to the customary standards of the Roman empire. They were not disloyal, lawless, or unpatriotic citizens or slaves, but they nevertheless now lived their lives according to a different law. They were even accused of being atheists because they refused to honor as divine the gods of the empire.

Within the world in which not even the Bible had questioned the legitimacy of slavery, based upon the unquestioned presupposition that nature itself had created some superior and others inferior, it is startling that the followers of the way of Galilee eventually broke with and distanced themselves from that mentality. They did not at first demand that the world change its laws, but within its confines it started to live a life that was in sharp contradiction to that of the state. All men and women were children

of the same God. Within the church, master and slave, citizen and foreigner, men, women, and children, were admitted to the catechumenate, the
agapes, the sacraments, on a basis of equality. One could even become "superior" to one's former "superiors"—the slave Callixtus became pope.

And even more. The most important Christians were not those who were
powerful and could easily take care of themselves. It was the beggars, the
lame, the sick, the abandoned, the foreigner, the disfigured, the slaves, and
all the faceless and voiceless "nobodies" of the world who were the privileged members. The church did not formulate a socio-political system, but
the seeds of future democracies wherein all would be respected and treated
alike were certainly present in the life of the way of Galilee.

From the very beginning, without wanting to be a political body, the
church posed a threat to the state because it refused to accept the state as
divine. Political organization is necessary, but it is not God. It must rule and
legislate, but it must itself submit to a greater ruler and legislator. And the
goal of the state must be the good and protection of all, especially those in
greatest need.

In speaking about itself, the church uses such terms as *mystery* and *people of God.*[2] It is incarnated in the world, but not swallowed up by it. It
expresses itself through the language and symbols of the people, but its
message revolutionizes the meaning of both the language and the symbols.
The church is the *mestizo par excellence* because it strives to bring about a
new synthesis of the earthly and the heavenly (Eph. 1:10). It is the "third"
or new people, which assumes the good that was there before and gives it
new meaning, direction, and life: faith, hope, and charity.

Mestizaje as Prophetic Mission

As a Galilean confronting Jerusalem, Jesus confronted a structured system to which at the same time he did and he did not belong: he was not one
of the in-group, but neither was he a total outsider. In his Galilean identity,
he questioned the official structures. But still, he was a Jew; he questioned
the system from within. That is what provoked the anger and opposition of
those in command—the inner core of Jewish society. As an insider questioning the absolutized structures, he endangered their security. He assailed
their hypocrisy, their use of religion to oppress the people. And he offered
the people something new and unexpected. In the name of their God, he
questioned their own understanding of God. To the establishment this was
blasphemy!

As a Galilean he demonstrates the role of a marginal person who by reason of being marginal is both an insider and an outsider—partly both, yet
fully neither. And he is not just trying to get into the structures, but to
change the structures in such a way that no one will be kept out, segregated,
dehumanized, or exploited. The role of questioning the structures will fall

upon those who are sufficiently "in" to know how the structures work, but likewise sufficiently "out" to know by personal experience that the structures are not working well and need to be liberated.

This is a ministry to be exercised by in/out-groups in all places and times. They are the "third," the new, people of today's world. Because they have been "in" and "out" of two systems, they will have new alternatives to offer to both. They will have the necessary intimacy with and distance from both establishments to be able to denounce the bad and point out the good in both systems. As such they have a liberative and creative task in the service of themselves and of their parent groups.

In following the divine mandate, we must not limit ourselves to confronting the *others* with their faults against *us*. This would be easy and would quickly win us the acclaim of our own people for we all like to hear how good we are at the expense of how bad the others are. This is true racism: to see oneself as essentially good while seeing the other as essentially evil. We must, as followers of Jesus, confront evil *wherever* its dehumanizing and disfiguring power is at work. This means confronting the evil ways not just of the others, but likewise of our own people.

It is true that the dominant society of both Mexico and the U.S.A. has treated Mexican-Americans unjustly, and these injustices must be denounced as sinful, or even diabolical. However we Mexican-Americans also destroy ourselves from within. There are many beautiful aspects of our Latin American Catholic culture. But like all human cultures, it too is impregnated with sin—sin that becomes so ordinary that we fail to perceive it as destructive of life itself.

The Mexican-American poor have to challenge the Latin American rich to be more responsive to the needs of the poor. In this, we have much to learn from our Calvinist brothers and sisters for whom wealth was a sign of blessing but also of social responsibility. The great problem posed by the Latin American rich is that for them wealth appears only as a blessing, not also as a responsibility. They easily and without any qualms of conscience squander their money on trips, jewelry, cars, sumptuous meals, and palatial homes while ignoring and exploiting the poor of their society. They despise the poor and ignore their misery.

There is hardly any *social consciousness* among wealthy Latin Americans. They see themselves "superior" by nature and not responsible for the misery of "inferior" human beings. There are no Latin American family foundations for the financing of social projects. They must be challenged. The gospel must be announced clearly by the Latin American poor so as to liberate the rich from their empty and artificial lives that are being wasted away in the process of their own damnation.

There is a great sense of national and cultural pride and unity among us Mexican-Americans, but we cannot unite for common projects. Our indomitable individualism and absolutism destroy our common efforts. Each one of us insists on having the last word and there is no room for compromise. If someone compromises, he or she is considered a "sell-out"—*un vendido*. It is noteworthy that there is no word for "compromise" in Mexican-American Spanish. We do not need the Anglo or anyone else to divide us, for we quickly and easily divide ourselves and rip each other apart. As long as we can keep blaming the Anglo society for all our misfortunes, we will never advance. The truth is that there is evil on both sides—in the dominant group and in ourselves. But it is much easier to blame the other than to face ourselves. To face our limitations openly is essential to liberation. This works both ways, for the dominant society would likewise prefer to put the entire blame on the poor, the marginated, and the foreigner rather than admit that they themselves are largely to blame for the sufferings of those living in misery.

Our beautiful Indian trait of indirect communication can degenerate into an obstacle to communication. Often we Mexican-Americans are so over-careful about not offending the other that we never tell them what needs to be said. Thus at meetings we all agree with each other—but cut each other's throat as soon as we leave the session. Without losing that deep personal strength that allows us to be gentle and calm even in the most trying and difficult circumstances, we must learn how to disagree openly with each other without taking personal offense. We must learn that we can disagree without being disagreeable.

Our deep sense of honor and family unity sometimes leads us to unrestrained vengeance. If someone in our family has been offended, we are convinced that we have a blood obligation to avenge their honor. This leads to family feuds, fights, and murders. Our usual politeness and warmth can quickly turn into unsuspected forms of violence.

In confronting our own cultural situation with truth, we Mexican-Americans should not make the mistake of just trading our way of life for the "American way." That would be a grave error. The American way of life is also in need of purification. Americans cannot just stand around silently and uncritically when they become aware of the failure of their systems, which are destroying them from within as a people and destroying many of the poorer countries of the world through various types of exploitation.

American monolingualism must be confronted. English is here to stay as the language of the U.S.A., but why must Americans be underdeveloped in relation to other peoples of the world in their ability to understand and speak other languages? Bilingualism is not an impoverishment but an enrichment. The more languages we know, the richer we are, because we can enjoy the beauty and expressiveness of diverse peoples. When bilingual education is asked for in American schools, it need not be thought of as a "concession" to "underdeveloped" Spanish-speaking pupils, but as an *enrichment opportunity* for all pupils (and others) in the school. From there the transition to other languages would be much easier.

Mexican-American efforts for bilingual education are often misunderstood and condemned, but such educational programs are one of the necessary roads to a future world fellowship. It is only through personal communication and friendship that Americans will move away from their self-taught xenophobia to the possibility of solidarity and cooperation with others. Languages are one of the important elements for the world community of tomorrow, which will not be monolingual but multilingual. As more and more peoples around the world learn each others' languages, it becomes more and more disastrous for the U.S.A. to lag behind.

The deification of breathless, ever upward mobility in American business and social life must be confronted. Many Americans are destroyed in the process of trying to make it to the top, and they destroy others, including family members, along the way. Such an attitude makes friendships impossible, for other persons are seen as potential competitors. Competition becomes the rule of life, and the Cain-Abel dynamic becomes deeper and more sophisticated. In modern American society, if one is not rushing to the top, one is considered to be tailspinning. The American value system needs to incorporate acceptance of reasonable limits to personal growth and of a graceful stability somewhere between having nothing and having everything. Happiness should be sought in obtaining what one really *needs*, without feeling impelled to scramble to the top—to the accompaniment of nervous disorders, heart attacks, strokes, and an early death.

The material comforts of modern North American civilization are not bad, but it must be admitted that in many ways they have turned into a curse. They consume consumers more than consumers consume them. Americans work, slave, and go into debt in order to keep on buying things they do not need. They have become entrapped by the very things they have produced. They no longer dominate the earth; the earth dominates them. In their quest for material prosperity and happiness, they no longer have time for contemplative leisure, for persons, and for themselves.

The Latin American sense of the primacy of the person and of human friendships could certainly confront this materialistic attitude and offer a liberating alternative. It is not material things and artificial beauty that will bring happiness into a person's life, but the discovery and enjoyment of authentic friendships—with persons who will accept me as I am, love me, and respect me simply because I am myself. It is not more *things* that will save the world, but more *love*, which will allow the overabundance of the goods we already possess to be more equitably distributed. To be free from the excess needs that we have created for ourselves will allow us to be free for that which is truly most important: other persons.

Americans long for intimacy and belonging, but their sense of rugged individualism with the freedom to "do my thing" does not allow either. Because they want to be in control of their intimacy and of the extent to which they will allow others to be in possession of them, they get more and more books on these subjects, and practice more and more techniques, only to become more and more frustrated. They want to remain in perfect control and yet be free. They go to therapy, transcendental sessions, nude encounters, giant crib sessions, Jesus-meetings, and whatever else comes along. They analyze themselves and put themselves in contact with the deeper ego. They can tell you all about themselves, but still experience deep aloneness and alienation. They want to enter into lasting and loving relationships, but are afraid to let go. They are afraid to surrender control. What they want the most they will not obtain, because they are afraid to die to their extreme individualism. The rugged cowboy in them must die if they are to experience the personal interdependence that will give them the intimacy and belonging that we all want.

We Mexican-Americans, in our Latin American sense of *familia* and *carnalismo* (brotherhood), have a great contribution to make. The *familia* gives its members a deep sense of security because they experience that they are someone special: loved, desired, valued, and respected simply because they are who they are—not because of what they ought to be or could become, but simply because they are who they are. No masks or games are necessary, for no matter what happens, one belongs. *La familia* is not the house where people reside; it is the bond that unites persons and allows them to experience that innermost and existential sense of belonging. I am never alone; I am part of the *familia* and the *familia* is part of me. Intimacy is natural because it is the ordinary behavior from the first to the last days of life—we touch, we joke, we caress, we converse . . . we can cry and sing, fight and love . . . yet in spite of everything, we are the *familia*.

Racism and Liberal Capitalism

There are two structural problems in the U.S.A. that particularly need to be confronted as far-ranging expressions of the sin of the world: racism and liberal capitalism. As brown-skinned and Spanish-speaking, we Mexican-Americans have experienced the pain of being rejected, segregated, and labeled inferior. Today we need to enter into solidarity with the blacks and the native peoples of North America to combat the racism of the U.S.A. and of Western civilization.

White Western supremacy permeates our way of life to such a degree that even good persons act in racist ways without even realizing that they are being racist. That is the tragedy of the social blindness of North American society. Racism and ethnocentrism are interwoven in literature, entertainment, institutions, marriage relations, finances, and even religious symbolism. This racist culture continues to bombard the nonwestern and nonwhite with the message that they are nonhuman. This is not said in so many words, but the message is loud and clear through all the media of communication.

The historical, social, economic, and religious roots of racism must be exposed and its present-day expressions and functions brought out into the light. Aggressive affirmative action programs must be instituted. They will never be popular because in themselves such programs are distasteful for everyone. Yet given the disastrous situation in which we all are living, such programs are urgently needed. Racism is a crime against the Creator and against the creatures made to the image and likeness of the Creator. It is an injustice, a sin.

And, as powerless as we Mexican-Americans might appear to be within the overall American population, we should not be afraid to confront and question that sacred cow of the Western world: liberal capitalism. My suggestion is not that we opt for Marxism. That would mean simply to trade one form of enslavement for another. But we do need to question critically the snowballing unemployment, inflation, and poverty that liberal capitalism is producing for the masses—both in the U.S.A. and around the world.

It becomes more and more evident that "development" means material advancement for fewer and fewer persons at the cost of material impoverishment for more and more. Development for a few means underdevelopment for many. The communications media project copious images of the "good life," but it is something that only a very minute percentage of the world population can have. Furthermore, with increased computerization and technological sophistication of production, the prevailing system will accelerate unemployment and impoverishment. An ever greater portion of the world's wealth will be controlled and enjoyed by an ever smaller percentage of the world's inhabitants.

Mexican-American Christians must enter into solidarity with the poor of other parts of the world in their struggles for a radically new humankind—the "third people." We are coming to the end of "the modern age."

There is no easy or obvious solution to this momentous and many-faceted problem. But its reality must be exposed. The consciousness and conscience of well intentioned persons must be quickened. Christian professionals, scholars, engineers, and scientists must search for creative ways for a new world civilization that does not build for a few at the cost of the many. The challenge is enormous; refusal to take up the challenge will be enormously disastrous. The answer does not lie in re-creating something which appeared to be successful in the past; it lies in bold and innovative searching and planning for a new future. Previously unimagined ways must be discovered if humankind is not simply to survive, but to become more human in the twenty-first century.

The Throne of the Liberator: The Cross

In determining to go to Jerusalem, Jesus accepted the more difficult part of his mission. In order to work for liberation and peace, it is not enough to work quietly among the grassroots; one must be willing to confront injustice. It is not enough to proclaim the kingdom; one must be willing to denounce the satanic powers present and operative in unjust socio-cultural and political structures. This is exactly what Pope John Paul II is doing. He is speaking clearly about the evils of both Marxism and capitalism. He is speaking against the evil of totalitarian systems that destroy the dignity of the human person.

It will never be easy to go to the centers of the establishment—*any* establishment—with the word of truth. What happened to Jesus will continue to happen to those who dare to speak the prophetic word today. The structures will react violently to silence them. This is an everyday occurrence in the "Catholic continent" of Latin America. The powerful, who not infrequently claim to be Catholic, are contemptuous of these "useless dreamers, gripers, troublemakers, rabblerousers, foreigners, communist agitators, revolutionaries. . . ." The prophetic voice is silenced or discredited because it exposes the exploitation of the Indian and of the masses of the poor throughout the continent.

No matter how carefully the poor act within the law, when they make their grievances and their hopes known to those in control, the establishment will feel threatened and will react with anger and violence. The high and mighty appear astonished and scandalized: "After all we have done for them . . . where is their gratitude? Why can't they stay *in their place*—where God has put them? Imagine the audacity of these people; they come out and insult us, the decision-makers and leaders of society!" It is good "law and order" to keep the poor illiterate and domesticated.

In Christ, a Galilean people goes its way to be rejected and killed as upstarts and troublemakers—because they want to bring in healing, renewal, and peace. The establishment, even sometimes the ecclesiastical establishment, asks them: "Why do you come to disturb things and ask annoying questions? We have a neat organizational setup to allow "Christianity" and society to function together effectively and in an orderly way. Everything is under control and it has served us well. Who are you to come and question us? If you don't like what you see, go back to where you came from. We know what is best for you. Just listen to us and do it our way, and you too can be almost as good as we are." And once again, in this type of attitude, the condemnatory words of the establishment at Jerusalem are repeated: "It is better that one man die for the people" (John 11:50).

In forcing a Galilean people to take the place it assigns them, the establishment forces Jesus to take the place it assigns him. In silencing the voice of the "little ones" and getting rid of them, the establishment puts Jesus to death all over again (recall the identification revealed to St. Paul between the members of the Galilean church he was persecuting and the risen Lord: Acts 9:1–5). The establishment cannot find any place for them but the cross—the continuation of a crucified existence. But in so doing, the establishment only confirms the charges that Christ in his followers makes against it. The system itself shows publicly that the accusation against it of violence and oppression is indeed correct.

The challenge to us Mexican-American Christians is not to try to become like some other people—Mexican or American—but to bring their better elements into the birth of a new people, a new creation. It will be through the mechanisms of forging a new, more cosmopolitan, and Spirit-imbued identity that new life will begin to unfold. It must be worked at critically, creatively, and persistently, for the temptation will always be there to simply adopt one of the socio-national models readily available. The temptation will always be there to restore the old kingdom rather than labor to usher in the new kingdom of God.

We Mexican-Americans must take the risks involved in initiating new ways of life that will eliminate some of the dehumanizing elements of the present situation. We know that we will not eliminate all of them, and we know that what we will achieve will not come about easily or without much effort, organization, and frustration. But there is no other way to introduce new forms and new institutions that will perpetuate some of the best of the past while eliminating some of the worst. We will not build the perfect society, but we must do what is in us to at least build a better one.

The Mexican-American people celebrates the crucifixion of Jesus because his cross makes their cross meaningful and purposeful. It is not a fatalism that attracts them to the cross but an awareness of Jesus' determination to accept the way ordained by the Father: Jerusalem must be confronted. And modern Jerusalems must be confronted if liberation is to come about today: there is no alternative.

The masses know about the past and the future—a painful past and a glorious future. The present time is the time of the divine mission—mandate—to go to Jerusalem carrying the burden of the cross with hope.

The various movements for liberation and betterment are our divine must—our way to Jerusalem of today's world. We cannot back away or weaken. With Jesus and in his power, we must risk everything and go all the way, even to the Cross!

Chapter 9

THE RESURRECTION PRINCIPLE

Your grief will be turned into joy
[John 17:20].

The political and religious establishment celebrated what it saw as the utter defeat of Jesus. His own followers had accepted it with sorrow and hopelessness. They were leaving Jerusalem in total disappointment. As far as all were concerned, everything was finished. But then something very extraordinary and unexpected took place. It was revealed to them that he was alive.

Jesus was alive, and more—he was now immune to the ordinary restrictions of earthly existence. He was now much more closely and creatively present to them than before. The struggle of the carpenter's son from Galilee against the powers of Jerusalem was now shown to have been victorious. In victory, the road to Jerusalem now was seen as the only way for the true liberation of humanity.

The Paradox of Death unto Life

Humiliated by the world, Jesus was now exalted by God. If his name had been ridiculed by society, it was now extolled by God above all other names.

The encounter with the risen Lord was a transforming and illuminating experience. It threw a new light not only on the way of Jesus but also on his identity and mission—and on the identity and mission of his followers. They were no longer ashamed or afraid to be who they were. The cross, which until then had been a symbol of reprobation, now became a symbol of divine election.

We arrive thus at the third principle of interpretation and re-creation, the *resurrection principle:* only love can triumph over evil, and no human power can prevail against the power of unlimited love. Out of suffering and death, God will bring health and life. The more that the sinful world tries to crush and destroy the ways of unstinted love, the greater will be love's triumph. A Spanish *dicho* can be applied here: *no hay mal que por bien no venga* ("there is no evil from which good cannot come").

115

The joy experienced in this new life is so profound, so intense, and so visible that it cannot be kept hidden. It must be communicated. Mary ran to tell Peter and the others that she had seen the Lord. The apostles and early Christians knew they had to go out and let others know the good news of what they had experienced. Joy and the cause of joy *must* be communicated. The cause of their joy was precisely that Jesus, the crucified one, had indeed triumphed. He had risen from the dead.

Not only was this deeply felt joy the beginning of the proclamation of the good news, it was also the beginning of the disciples' search for the ultimate meaning of Jesus and his way through the world. From the ending of his life they would now seek to trace back his every step, his origins, even his genealogies.

The disciples' deep joy was the heartfelt joy that comes from profound and transforming experiences, which in turn give rise to ultimate certitude and conviction about the full meaning and direction of life itself. It was this joy that would allow them to meet head-on and without hesitation all opposition and even persecution. Even death would neither destroy them nor diminish the new life of the spirit that was now present and expanding. The end was ensured, and no human power could stop it.

The witness of the church from the earliest days to the present moment has certainly been consistent on this point. Wherever men and women of faith have given their lives for the sake of the kingdom, the church has grown and expanded.

One of the most revolutionary aspects of Christianity was that it introduced into the world a concept of hero diametrically opposed to anything the world had ever conceived of before then. The new hero was not the one who overpowered by physical force or who conquered others and built great empires. The new heros were the persons who in the power of the Lord were now strong enough to give their own life for the sake of their faith. They appeared weak in the eyes of worldly wisdom, but they challenged the wise and intelligent of the world as they had never been challenged before. The weapons of this world were useless against them, and even in death they radiated an inner peace and joy that worldly wisdom had never been able to achieve. Their new life of unlimited love, of loving others as God had loved them, was indeed a new life-form, such as the world had never before experienced.

This type of witness continues today. It continues in the vast regions of Latin America, where thousands of persons are giving their lives for the sake of the kingdom. Totalitarian dictatorships there are using physical and psychological torture to try to stop or get rid of them, but they will not succeed in stifling the power of the spirit. If anything, the more they oppose it, the more they will guarantee its ultimate success.

Nothing can substitute for the witness of Christian life. It is the way we live the new life of the spirit that will allow us to be a light in the darkness and the salt that brings out latent savor. We must clearly choose to be in the world but not of the world. As Onesimus, we must turn from enslavement—from the multiple enslavements of this world—to discover in those emarginated by the world what it means to be a child of God (see Paul's Letter to Philemon).

Persons who enter the religious life have always seen the need to withdraw from the enslavements of the world through a freely chosen life of poverty, chastity, and obedience. But there are also those whom the world has pushed out onto the margins of society. They are not enslaved by worldly affairs: they have never been allowed to take part in them. The ones who are the furthest away from the centers of belonging and acceptability will be the first ones to see the empty tomb and encounter the risen Lord.

The Dry Bones Come to Life (Ezekiel 37)

The poor and marginated of society can be transformed in their encounter with the risen Lord. In him, they can come to life and overcome their fears. They will no longer be enslaved or silenced, nor will they hide away in their ghettos. As the "new" Galileans of the Acts of the Apostles, they will not hesitate to speak openly and make the truth be heard by all. Concrete manifestations of sin will be exposed. Such denunciations are part of the divine mandate constitutive of discipleship of Jesus on his way to Jerusalem. In the encounter with the risen Lord, the powerless of society are now reborn so as to become a new power for the salvation of all.

But it is not so much any one person who is called upon to pursue this confrontation as the community of believers, those who recognize that their gift of poverty and margination is given to them precisely to act as the agents of liberation for the entire group—powerful and powerless alike.

Community Organization—And Revivification

This is exactly what is beginning to happen in various community organizations in some of the key American urban centers where there are heavy concentrations of Spanish-speaking peoples—San Antonio, Chicago, Los Angeles. It is also taking place in rural areas among farm workers. Unions and community organizations are being formed among the poor and powerless of society so that, by working together on the issues that affect the life of the group, their powerlessness may be turned into a new type of power that will confront the powerful of society in order to bring about necessary changes for the benefit of all.

The mission that these groups are living out is the nonviolent unveiling of injustices hidden and functioning in the American way of life. Through organizations such as the United Farm Workers, COPS of San Antonio, UNO of Los Angeles, and TON of Chicago, the voiceless now have a voice and the powerless now have a power. Those who had been counted for nothing are now being recognized as somebody.

Christian Base Communities

The new resurrection-life is evidenced most clearly in the Christian base communities *(comunidades de base)* that are flourishing throughout Latin America, especially in the areas of greatest poverty. "Ordinary persons" are discovering themselves to be renewed, truly children of God, as they come into direct contact with God's word, pray together, seek to serve the common good together, and celebrate their faith.

As simple as this might sound, its truly revolutionary consequences are astronomical. It will truly turn things inside out and begin a new social order. There is no greater threat to any unjust system—regardless of what ideological titles it might use to identify itself—than persons who have been transformed in the Lord and thus have become aware of their fundamental human dignity and that of all others. Such an awakening is nothing less than a rebirth unto new life.

This rebirth, while not itself political or economic, will pose the deepest questions, challenges, and threats to any system that is built upon and perpetuates inequality. Revitalized Christians are no longer afraid to die for what they believe in, for they know with the certitude of the faith-encounter that there is more to life than the threat of death, and that even torture and death cannot quench the Spirit. Because they have discovered life, they are no longer afraid to die.

What happened in Nicaragua and what is happening in Brazil, El Salvador, and other parts of Latin America appear to be no less miraculous or phenomenal than the spread and consequences of early Christianity itself. When the poor, the oppressed, and the marginated become aware of who they are in the Lord and begin their struggle for humanization, then the true liberation of humanity has begun. No matter how slow and difficult it might be, no matter how many are martyred or maimed, liberation will succeed, because no human power can keep Jesus in the tomb, no human power will prevent the risen Lord from triumphing over the powers of evil. Not with the weapons of destruction will the converted poor triumph, but with the weapons of the power of selflessness and truth in the service of love.

An important element of this new power is that it is not power for the sake of personal gain, but power for the sake of all the oppressed, ignored, forgotten, and exploited members of society. The powerless are recouping power, but it is not the power of this world, which works for self-gain, but the power of the gospel, which works for the betterment and liberation of all, especially those in greatest need.

In all this, prophecy is not just being spoken about; it is being lived out in ongoing confrontations by the previously powerless of society who now dare to go to the Jerusalems of today's society: city hall, transnational corporations, boards of education, ecclesiastical offices. Those who had before simply accepted their state of exclusion and exploitation are now coming out of their tombs of substandard housing, disease-infected neighborhoods, economically enslaving jobs, schools that strengthened illiteracy, and churches that perpetuated segregation. Those who had been dead are now coming back to life.

In this awakening and coming back to life, renewed Christians are called to exercise a prophetic role. True prophecy is based upon a prophetic lifestyle, which of itself—wordlessly—confronts an ungodly society. It is this new lifestyle—this new way of relating with persons, goods, institutions, and God—that is itself an arresting alternative to the ways of the world.

Thus, the main confrontation posed by Jesus was not necessarily his head-on arguments with the authorities, but the living out of a new lifestyle of fellowship with all others. It was Jesus' practice of table-fellowship with all kinds of persons, including the despised of society, that most pointedly confronted the system and pricked the sensitivities of the accepted "solid citizens" of his society. Actions speak louder than words, and prophetic actions speak louder than prophetic words. Jesus did not speak about desegregation as such, but he joyfully lived it out as one of the most distinctive characteristics of his earthly life. He did not hesitate to castigate the rich, the proud, the well educated, the religious, and the powerful. But he was patient, merciful, and understanding with the sick, the poor, the ignorant, and the errant. The living out of this new relationship with all others—with the world and with God—confronted the institutionalized ideology of the early church's social environment, and constituted the basis of the ongoing confrontation of Christianity with the world and its powers.

It must be stated clearly that Jesus and Christians today are not prophets of doom but bearers of good news. If the good news sounds bad for some, it is because it draws attention to something amiss. But the good element in such a disclosure is that Jesus offers a cure. The ultimate bad news would be if the sickness was never diagnosed and no cure sought, thus ensuring death. Jesus condemns the sickness of the world and offers it health, salvation. Even in condemnation, there is good news! You can repent and be saved. Something radically new is offered. It is this radical newness that the converted poor and marginated continue to offer to the world at every moment of history.

Joy That Transcends Divisions

Mestizaje as Festive Prophecy

For prophecy to be truly Christian, it cannot stop at confrontation and denunciation. The fullness of Christian prophecy, which is not just the road to earthly Jerusalems but even beyond them to the heavenly Jerusalem, includes the festive celebrations of the inception of the heavenly Jerusalem here and now.

One of the greatest things the Christian has to offer our mixed-up and alienated world is that, while realistically facing the struggles of life, one can rise above them and experience and radiate authentic joy and hope, peace and serenity. It is in the celebrations of what has indeed begun but is yet to come in its fullness that the Christian announces the kingdom already in existence in our midst and nourishes the faith that enables followers of Jesus to endure even the cross.

The prophetic without the festive turns into cynicism and bitterness, or simply fades away. On the other hand, the festive without the prophetic can easily turn into empty rituals or even degenerate into drunken brawls. It is the prophetic-festive that keeps the spirit alive and nourishes the life of the group as a group. Moses was well aware of this when he commanded that the original and originating events of the Jewish people be celebrated annually. The Christian community was aware of it when it went on celebrating what had been most original in the way of Jesus: radical forgiveness that flowed into the joy of table-fellowship with all persons. For living out this prophetic action Jesus had been crucified by human beings, but raised by God. It was in the joy of this heartfelt forgiveness that reintegrates the outcast into the community, the joy that comes with the awareness that you are accepted and valued simply because you are you, that the Christians celebrated the death and resurrection of Jesus that had brought about this new communitarian life transcending human frontiers and institutions. The celebrations of the originating events kept the group alive, thankful and joyful even in the midst of the most cruel persecutions. There was a power in those celebrations that human powers could neither grasp nor destroy.

The joy of Mexican-Americans is one of their most obvious characteristics. They love their fiestas and everyone is welcome to participate. Neither destitution nor wars can dampen their festive spirit. Even in the midst of suffering, there is a spontaneous joy that is not easily found elsewhere. Outsiders notice it and comment upon it. It is obvious in liturgical gatherings, spontaneous in home life, and carefully planned into commemorations of historical events. In their sorrows, disappointments, reverses, and struggles, there is joy. It is evident in the eyes and smiles of their children, in the playfulness of their youth, and in the inner peace and tranquility of their elderly. In the midst of whatever happens—triumph or tragedy—they rise above it to celebrate life.

It cannot be adequately explained but it can certainly be sensed, for it is nothing less than the joy of the experience of new life within them—not yet fully realized but certainly beginning. It is through the ongoing synthesis of traditions that this new life is gradually coming into its fullness.

The Fiesta of Group Origins

Through the celebration of the foundational events that had brought the group into existence, the people not only continued the life of the group as group, but deepened the full meaning and implications of the very significance and mission of their new existence.

The festive celebrations of their origins transcended time and space, and allowed those present here and now—wherever and whenever the "here and now" might be—to enter vicariously into the founding events of the group. These celebrations also projected the participants confidently into the future because they allowed them to taste what was yet to come.

When the founding events of the group are reactualized in celebrations, the beginning and the end are both present in the festive now. These collective celebrations are both re-creative of the group and supportive of its growth and continuation. They are the experiential way of passing on the core knowledge of the originality of the group, not just in a cerebral way but in a truly existential way.

One can have extensive knowledge about a group, but if personal experience is missing, one does not *belong*. *Members* belong because they have experienced what is original to them. Whether they verbalize it or not, they know they belong! They have experienced what has brought them into existence and distinguished them from other human groups.

It is through these foundational celebrations that the core knowledge of the group functions and is passed on as living tradition and the fundamental myths of the group take shape and are articulated. Without these celebrations, it is simply the remembrance of a historical past, but not the appreciation of a past that lives in the present, transforming it into a future that has already begun. In this way, celebrations are not just the effects of what has been; they are likewise the cause of what is yet to come. Yet without the religious myths to explain the core symbols of the group, celebrations of origins degenerate into mere nostalgic happenings, which cease to nourish the life of the group.

The experience that the first disciples had received from the Lord himself they passed on to new converts through words and gestures. For the universal Christian community, the foundational experience is the life of Jesus who had been crucified but then raised from the dead by God. Newcomers shared this foundational experience in their death-through-baptism and in the *agape* of table-fellowship. This is especially brought out at Pentecost, when the church as church celebrates its origination and its originality. Those who had been strongly nationalistic and ghetto-minded now became aware that they had to go beyond their own nationalistic, linguistic, and geographical belonging.

In the context of their celebrations, they experienced and reexperienced what was most original about Jesus—everyone is welcome! Thus the church grew not as a result of intellectually convincing arguments, but as the result of a new joyful experience from which new knowledge and institutions would gradually emerge. But it was precisely in celebration that individuals transcended their own intellectual hang-ups or cultural prejudices and were able to experience the other as other. It was there that cultural masks disappeared and the beauty of the other as other was able to shine forth for all to see and appreciate. This discovery was at the core of the easily recognizable joy so characteristic of the Christian community. And it was this joy that both denounced the pleasures of a joyless society and announced new possibilities of happiness heretofore unsuspected.

The new creation today begins not as a result of logical thinking or planning, but as the consequence of the new joy of being, experienced above all else in the fiestas of the poor and the rejected. It is there that even the most powerful of the world can forget the labels that they think one has to "live up to"; they can simply be themselves. It is likewise there that the despised can ignore the labels that proclaim them to be inferior and rise to the full stature of their being. It is in the truly Christian fiesta—the *agape*—that all experience themselves for what they truly are: children of the same father, without need for distinctions or explanations. In these moments of togetherness, we relativize the human barriers that keep us apart and we celebrate the unity of the earthly with the celestial.

If the poor can celebrate as can no one else, it is precisely because, being deprived of the goods of this world, they are very aware of the one gift that alone counts—awareness that God lives among us and has especially chosen us to be the bearers of the good news of salvation. Everyone else might reject us but it makes little difference when we know that God has chosen us to be his messengers.

The fiestas of the poor are truly celebrations: the poor have a *reason* to celebrate. Hence their celebrations are joyful, free, and spontaneous, whereas the celebrations of the rich tend to be more of a tedious chore than a spontaneous joy. They appear to be having a good time while inwardly they are worrying about wearing the right outfit, saying the right things, doing the right things, mixing with the right persons, and impressing everyone around with the multiple masks that everyone puts on to impress the others. In effect, the celebrations of the "dignitaries" of this world are anything but joyful. How could they be joyful when they are segregated and segregating, and potentially destructive of all who take part in them?

Thus it is out of the celebrations of the poor, which will always be a scandal to the rich who are not capable of truly liberative celebrations, that God's universal and barrier-destroying love will erupt for all to experience and enjoy. Participants will rise above what enslaves them and will experience the full liberation of the children of God. They can truly be themselves because they are "at home" in the household of the father—no masks to put on, no "higher-ups" to impress, no jealousies to worry about. In this joy, we have a foretaste of a final result of the plenary fellowship of humanity. Having experienced the end, we will begin working to make it more of a reality in today's world.

The Fiesta of Christian Birth

For the Mexican-American Christian community, the foundational experience is the death brought about by foreign conquests and the new life begun when God raised up a wondrous sign: *la Morenita del Tepeyac.* As the universal church celebrates its foundational experience on pentecost, so the Mexican-American Christian community celebrates its foundational experience as a local church on the feast of Our Lady of Guadalupe, December 12. And just as millions of baptisms followed the first December 12, so it is today that through baptism new members enter into the local church—not a different church but the universal church present in this particular space and time.

In the celebration of Our Lady of Guadalupe, we Mexican-Americans celebrate the common mother of all the inhabitants of the Americas. As it was the ones in greatest need, the despised and rejected Galileans, who first experienced the unlimited and compassionate love of the Father through Jesus, so it was the ones in greatest need at the time of the birth of the Americas, the conquered and despised Indians, who first experienced the unlimited and compassionate love of the mother of God. In the power of the Spirit, the Galileans saw that the manifestation of Christian love involved not only their own ethnic group but all the nations and cultures of the world. The Spirit led them to realize that they could not do to others what others had done to them. They could not impose their culture, their language, their ways, or even their religious practices, upon others.

As the Galileans went to share this newly discovered love with all others, so today Mexican-American Christians, in the power of the same Spirit, must carry their boundary-transcending experience of the common mother of all the inhabitants of Mexico to all the peoples of the Americas. The dynamics of the good news must continue in today's world: it is through the ignorant and powerless that salvation will come to the learned and powerful of this world (see 1 Cor. 26–31).

In the foundational experience of the universal Christian church the foundational experience of our own local church is clarified and ennobled. It is a fact that it was to the marginals from Galilee, the followers of Jesus, that the revelation of God's universal love was first given. By their very existence on the periphery of Jewish society, they had been less imprisoned by the system. This does not mean that the experience of the defeat of the old order led them immediately to a full understanding of the resurrection as the wellspring of unbarriered universalism and catholicism. The developing situations of the early church forced them to reflect again and again on the meaning of the foundational event, to try to understand it more deeply. The Spirit remained with them and the Lord continued to reveal himself in ongoing events. He was the Lord of history.

The new universalism of the Americas, which would slowly break through the barriers of caste and class, started among the "Galileans" of Mexican society of that time—the conquered Indians who lived on the periphery of power and civilization. It was through Juan Diego and the subjugated, despised Indians that the new creation would begin. Who was to tell them that they were to be the apostles of a new universalism? Our Lady of

Guadalupe has been the one to enable the Mexican and the Mexican-American peoples—*pueblos mestizos*—to reaffirm their integrity and liberate themselves from extraneous powers.

It is the mother of the Americas who today is the one to bring about a new creation in the Americas. No Christian today would think of denying Christ because he was a Galilean Jew, yet many American Christians ignore the mother of Jesus as she appeared in Tepeyac because she appeared as an Indian maiden. Yet her words were: "I am the mother of all the inhabitants of this land."

It is in the celebration of the common motherhood of all the inhabitants of these lands that Americans will be able to begin to break through the many barriers that continue to perpetuate a segregated society. To the degree that the powerful and proud can accept the common motherhood of the *mestiza* Virgin of Tepeyac, they will begin to take down the barriers they created to legitimate the exploitation of the "little ones" of society. It is in the living appreciation of the common motherhood of Mary the mother of Jesus and the mother of us all, as she chose to appear in this land that we call America, that class struggle will eventually disappear and a new *raza,* a new creation, will appear.

This joyful message of the common mother of all the inhabitants of this land will not be spread through words, for the rejects of society often do not have the proper words to express their thoughts and convictions. It will be proclaimed and transmitted through a much more universal language easily appreciated by anyone who experiences it: the festive celebrations of the people. It is in the fiesta that reality is experienced. Antagonisms and divisions are bypassed. It is in the fiesta that a new common "we" begins to be experienced. We belong together because we have experienced a new unity and universality. Eventually the words will be found to explain it, but in the meantime the new reality has begun to emerge.

From the very beginning Christianity saw itself living out a new universal love that would not be limited by cultural or religious boundaries. This new love came through many cultures (the way of the incarnation) but at the same time transcended them by opening them up to the wealth and riches of other cultures (the way of transcendence)—to respect local cultures but not to canonize new ghettos. This new love led to new marriages between persons who previously did not even look at each other, and these new marriages were blessed with new progeny. New ethnic groups came about that represented neither the victory nor the defeat of an established people, but a new creation.

Mestizaje is the beginning of a new Christian universalism. The depth of joy present in the *mestizo* celebration is indicative of the eschatological *mestizo* identity: they are the ones in whom the fullness of the kingdom has already begun, the new universalism that bypasses human segregative barriers.

But there is also a sense of pain and tragedy present in *mestizo* celebrations because what has already begun is neither accepted nor appreciated by the wisdom and power that largely rule over this world.

But for those who have eyes to see and ears to hear, the mestizo is the *gospel* in today's world: the proclamation in flesh and blood that the longed-for kingdom has in fact begun.

And so we Mexican-Americans celebrate the joy of what has begun in us, and we suffer the pain of the tragedy that the world has not yet discovered it. In our *posadas* we celebrate the real meaning of our identity that remains hidden to the eyes of those who will not see. In our personal devotion to *Diosito* we live in intimate communion with the ultimate source of life—an experience often absent from institutional catechesis, nonabrasive preaching, and ecclesiastical theology.

The Mexican-American celebration of suffering, especially on *Viernes Santo* and in *Jesús en la cruz,* often appears morbid to those who fear death and suffering. But to those whose daily life is suffering and death, only a suffering God on the cross can give meaning to the absurdities that life multiplies.

If the "enlightened" and "educated" scoff at Mexican-American devotion to the virgin mother, it is because they have never really experienced the joy of birth. In their devotion to *la Morenita,* Mexican-Americans celebrate the suffering of childbirth—not unto a creation manipulated and straightened by self-interested human designs, but unto a new creation open to the effusive dynamism of the Spirit.

Fiestas may be foolishness to those who seek rational discourse; they may be stumbling blocks to those who seek timely, logical, and efficient action. But to those who have participated in the collective mystical experience of Christian faith, they are a celebration of God's power unto new creation. They speak salvation to those who believe—the death unto life of a people . . . the joyful expression and visible sign of God's power unto new life.

NOTES

Introduction

1. *Mestizaje: The Dialectic of Cultural Birth and the Gospel. A Study in the Intercultural Dimension of Evangelization* (Paris: Institut Catholique; San Antonio: Mexican-American Cultural Center, 1978).

Part One

1. J. Ruffie, *De la biologie à la culture* (Paris: Flammarion, 1976), p. 233.

Chapter 1

1. As culled from various dictionaries, we can define racism: a belief that race is the primary determinant of human traits and capacities, and that racial differences produce an inherent superiority of a particular race.

2. M. Mörner, *Race Mixture in the History of Latin America* (Boston: Little, Brown, 1967), ch. 4, pp. 35–52.

3. For a fuller discussion, see V. Elizondo, *La Morenita—Evangelizer of the Americas* (San Antonio: Mexican-American Cultural Center, 1980), part 2, ch. 2–4, pp. 75–92.

4. See L. Poliakov, *Le mythe aryen* (Paris: Calmann-Lévy, 1971), p. 141.

5. See Martin Marty, *Righteous Empire: The Protestant Experience in America* (New York: Dial, 1976), pp. 5–13.

6. Ibid., pp. 5–13 and 24–33.

7. See M. S. Meier and F. Rivera, *The Chicanos: A History of Mexican-Americans* (New York: Hill & Wang, 1972), pp. 21–28.

8. G. W. Price, *Origins of the War with Mexico* (Austin: University of Texas Press, 1976), p. 4.

9. Price, *Origins,* p. vii.

10. See R. Acuña, *Occupied America* (San Francisco: Canfield, 1972); Thomas P. Fenton, *Education for Justice: A Resource Manual* (Maryknoll: Orbis Books, 1975); C. Hernandez, N. Wagner, and M. Haug, *Chicanos: Social and Psychological Perspectives* (St. Louis: Mosby, 1971); United States Commission on Civil Rights, *Mexican-American Education Study*, reports of 1971, 1972, and 1973.

11. The genetic make-up of the human being is most complex. Some have thought it possible to have only individuals of certain ideal traits produce children so as to develop a master race. Others have feared and guarded against race mixture for a fear of weakening the "race." These opinions are false and go against the findings of

contemporary science on the importance of bringing in new genes for the gradual strengthening of the total human race. According to French biologist J. Ruffié, the more pure, genetically speaking, a group is, the weaker it becomes. The so-called master race of Hitler would have in effect become the most fragile human group. Ruffié demonstrates how, biologically speaking, it is through race mixture that new genetic pools are introduced, thus strengthening and giving more vitality to the newly produced generation. Biologically speaking, race mixture is the natural way of perfecting and uniting the human being.

Biologically, race mixture is not only good, but even beneficial. The serious difficulties encountered by race mixture are not biological but social. It is not easy to be a *mestizo*, and societies whose sociological self-preservation instincts want their progeny to remain pure will reject the *mestizo* as the most serious threat to the continuity to the group. There is also the suffering entailed since *mestizaje* normally comes through conquest and political or military domination. The *mestizo* must then either assume the cultural way of life of the dominant group or be totally rejected. The ideal would be for the sociological reality to build upon the biological reality. Since it is through the synthesis of both that a new, stronger, and more perfect human species is produced so it would be not through conquest or elimination but through a cultural synthesis of the sociological characteristics of both groups that a new, more perfect, and more human society would evolve.

For scientific evidence on the biological and cultural advantages of *mestizaje,* I recommend strongly Ruffié's book *De la biologie à la culture* (Paris: Flammarion, 1976).

Chapter 2

1. On both these points, see Frank del Olmo, "Portrait of a Hero Slowly Emerges," syndicated article from the *Los Angeles Times*, February 2, 1981.

2. In numerous case histories studied by Sr. Augustine Weilbert, resident graphologist/psychologist at the Mexican-American Cultural Center, one of the most common traits discovered has been that of the very low self-esteem, very modest self-image, of the Mexican-American. Their own self-image—*"no sirvo para nada*; I'm not good for anything"—keeps them from developing their known capabilities.

3. R. Díaz-Guerrero, *Psychology of the Mexican: Culture and Personality* (Austin: University of Texas Press, 1975).

4. For example, the COPS (Citizens Organized for Public Service) in San Antonio, the Raza Unida party, the Chicano Manifesto, the farmworker movement in California, Texas, and elsewhere.

5. R. Duran, *Salubridad Chicana: Su preservación y mantenimiento. The Chicano Plan for Mental Health* (Denver: n.p., 1975).

Chapter 4

1. See W. D. Davies, *The Gospel and the Land* (Berkeley: University of California Press, 1974), p. 425.

2. E. Lohmeyer, *Galilee und Jerusalem* (Göttingen: Vandenhoeck & Ruprecht, 1936).

3. R.H. Lightfoot, *Locality and Doctrine in the Gospel* (New York, 1938).

4. W. Marxsen, *Der Evangelist Markus: Studien zur Redaktionsgeschichte des Evangeliums* (Göttingen: Vandenhoeck & Ruprecht, 1956).

5. W. Meeks, "Galilee and Judea in the Fourth Gospel," in *Journal of Biblical Literature* 85 (1966), No. 2, pp. 159–69.

6. L. E. Elliott-Binns, *Galilean Christianity* (London: SCM Press, 1956), p. 85.

7. Davies, *The Gospel*, p. 436.

8. J. Mateos, *Nuevo Testamento* (Madrid: Cristiandad, 1974), p. 736.

Chapter 5

1. M. Clevenot, *Approches matérialistes de la Bible* (Paris: Cerf, 1976), p. 98.

Chapter 6

1. D. A. Lane, *The Reality of Jesus* (New York: Paulist, 1975), p. 54.

Chapter 8

1. Tertullian, *Scorpiace*, 10, as quoted in R. A. Markus, *Christianity in the Roman World* (New York: Scribner's, 1974), p. 24.

2. Vatican II, *Lumen Gentium*, ch. 1 and 2.

Bibliography

Historical

Acuña, R. *Occupied America: The Chicano Struggle toward Liberation*. San Francisco: Canfield Press, 1972

Alba, V. *The Mexicans*. New York: Pegasus, 1967.

Bastide, R. *Anthropologie Appliquée*. Paris: Payot, 1971.

———. *Sociologie et psychologie*. Paris: PUF, 1972.

Chavarria, J. "La Causa Chicana: Revolution Yet to Come." *Origins* 4, no. 43 (April, 1975): 673-677.

———. "A Precise and Tentative Bibliography on Chicano History." *El Grito* (Spring, 1971): 133-141.

Cotera, M., and L. Hufford. *Bridging Two Cultures, Multidisciplinary Readings in Bilingual Bicultural Education*. Austin: National Educational Laboratory Publ., 1980.

Davis, K. "The Migrations of Human Populations." *Scientific America* 231, no. 3 (1974): 92.

Díaz-Guerrero, R. *Psychology of the Mexican: Culture and Personality*. Austin: University of Texas Press, 1975.

Duijker, H.C.J., and N.H. Frijda. *National Character and National Stereotypes*. Amsterdam: North Holland Publishing Co., 1960.

Duran, F.D. *Historia de las Indias de Nueva España y Islas de Tierra Firme*. Mexico: Editorial Nacional, 1967.

Duran, L.I., and H.R. Bernard. *Introduction to Chicano Studies*. New York: Macmillan, 1973.

Dussel, E. *History and the Theology of Liberation*. Maryknoll, New York: Orbis, 1976.

Dutton, B.P. *Indians of the American Southwest*. Englewood Cliffs, New Jersey: Prentice Hall, 1974.

Elizondo, V. *Christianity and Culture*. Huntington, Indiana: Our Sunday Visitor Press, 1975.

Forbes, J.D. *Aztecas del Norte*. Greenwich, Conn.: Fawcett Publications, Inc. 1973.

Garibay, K.A.M. *Historia de la literatura Nahuatl*. Mexico: Editorial Porrua, 1953-54.

———. *La literature de los Aztecas*. Mexico: Mortiz, 1964.

Gomez-Quinones, J. "Toward a Perspective on Chicano History." *El Grito* (Fall, 1971): 1-49.

Grebler, L., J.Moore, and R. Guzman. *The Mexican American People*. New York: The Free Press, 1970.

Guerrero, J.R. *Catecismos españoles del siglo XVI*. Madrid: Instituto Superior de Pastoral, 1969.

Hale, E.E. *How to Conquer Texas Before They Conquer Us*. Boston: Redding and Co., 1845.

Hammond, P.E. "The Sociology of American Civil Religion: A Bibliographic Essay." *Sociological Analysis* 37, no. 2 (Summer 1976): 169-182.

Hanke, L. *The Spanish Struggle for Justice in the Conquest of America.* Boston: Little, Brown and Company, 1965.

Hernandez, C., M. Haug, and N. Wagner. *Chicanos: Social and Psychological Perspectives.* 2nd ed. St. Louis: C.V. Mosby Co., 1976.

Josephy, A.M. *The Indian Heritage of America.* New York: Bantam Books, 1973.

Juárez, J.R. "La Iglesia Católica y el Chicano en Sud Texas, 1836-1911." *Aztlán: Chicano Journal of the Social Sciences and the Arts* 4, no. 2 (Fall, 1973).

Kirchner, L.O. *Mexico en busca de su identidad.* Madrid: Ediciones Iberoamericanas. S.A., 1973.

Lafaye, J. *Quetzalcóatl et Guadalupe.* Paris: Editions Gallimard, 1974.

Leon-Portilla, M. *Los Antiguos Mexicanos.* Mexico: Fondo de Cultura Ecónomica, 1972.

———. *Aztec Thought and Culture.* Norman: University of Oklahoma Press, 1963.

———. *El Reverso de la Conquista.* Mexico: Editorial Joaquin Mortiz, 1970.

———. *Visión de los Vencidos.* Mexico: UNAM, 1972.

Lucas, Isidro, *The Browning of America, The Hispanic Revolution in the American Church.* Chicago: Fides Claretian Press, 1981.

McCarthy, J. "Institutionalized Poverty." *National Council of Catholic Bishops, San Antonio Hearings.* Washington: United States Catholic Conference, 1975.

McWilliams, C. *North from Mexico.* New York: J.B. Lippencott, 1949.

Marienstras, E. *Les mythes fondateurs de la nation americaine.* Paris: Maspéro, 1976.

Marshall, C.E. "The Birth of the Mestizo in New Spain." *The Hispanic American Historical Review* 19 (1939).

Marty, M. *Righteous Empire: The Protestant Experience in America.* New York: The Dial Press, 1976.

Marty, M.E., and D.G. Peerman, eds. *New Theology no. 9: The New Particularisms.* New York: Macmillan, 1972.

Meier, M.S., and F. Rivera. *The Chicanos, A History of Mexican Americans.* New York: Hill and Wang, 1972.

———. *Readings on La Raza: The Twentieth Century.* New York: Hill and Wang, 1974.

Merk, F. *Manifest Destiny and Mission in American History: A Reinterpretation.* New York: Vintage Books, 1963.

Mörner, M. *Race Mixture in the History of Latin America.* Boston: Little, Brown and Co., 1967.

Murguia, E. *Assimilation, Colonialism and the Mexican American People.* Austin: The University of Texas Press.

Orozco, E.C. *Republican Protestantism in Aztlán.* The Petereins Press, 1980.

Phelan, J.L. *The Millenial Kingdom of the Franciscans in the New World: A Study of the Writings of Gerónimo de Mendieta, 1525-1606.* Berkeley: University of California Press, 1970.

Pitt, L. *The Decline of the Californios: A Social History of the Spanish Speaking Californios, 1846-1890.* Berkeley: University of California Press, 1966.

Poliakov, J. *Le Bréviaire de la haine, le Troisiéme Reich et les juifs.* Coll. "Le Livre de Poche." Paris: Calmann-Lévy, 1951.

———. *Histoire de l'Antisémitisme.* Paris: Calmann-Lévy, 1956-1977.

———. *Les Juifs et notre histoire.* Coll. "Science." Paris: Flammarion, 1973.

———. *Le Mythe aryen.* Paris: Calmann-Lévy, 1971.

———. *Le Racisme.* Paris: Seghers, 1976.

Price, G.W. *Origins of the War with Mexico.* Austin: University of Texas Press, 1976.

Ramírez, R. "The Church and the Hispanics in the Southwest." Paper delivered at the Mexican American Cultural Center in San Antonio, September 29, 1977.

Rosaldo, R., G. Seligmann, and R. Calvert. *Chicano: The Beginning of Bronze Power.* New York: William Morrow & Co., 1974.

Ruffie, J. *De la Biologie a la Culture.* Paris: Flammarion, 1976.

Ruiz, R.E. *The Mexican War: Was it Manifest Destiny?* New York: Holt, Rinehart and Winston, 1963.

de Sahagun, Fr. B. *Historia General de las cosas de Nueva España.* 4 vols. Mexico: Ed. Porrua, S.A., 1969.

Samora, J., and P.V. Simon. *A History of the Mexican-American People.* Notre Dame: University of Notre Dame Press, 1977.

Servin, M.P., ed. *The Mexican Americans: An Awakening Minority.* Beverly Hills, California: Glencoe Press, 1970.

Simpson, G.E., and J.M. Yinger. *Racial and Cultural Minorities.* New York: Harper, 1953.

Soustelle, J. *La Vida Cotidiana de los Aztecas.* Versión española de C. Villegas. Mexico City: Fondo de Cultura Económica, 1970.

Sylvest, E.E. *Motifs of Franciscan Mission Theory in Sixteenth Century New Spain Province of the Holy Gospel.* Washington: Academy of American Franciscan History, 1975.

Tamez, E. *The Bible of the Oppressed.* Maryknoll: Orbis, 1982.

Wagner, N., and M.J. Haug. *Chicanos: Social and Psychological Perspectives.* St. Louis: Mosby, 1971.

Socio-Cultural

Abrahams, R.D., and R.C. Troike. *Language and Culture Diversity in American Education.* Englewood Cliffs, New Jersey: Prentice Hall, 1972.

Acuña, R. *Occupied America: The Chicano Struggle toward Liberation.* San Francisco: Canfield Press, 1972.

Allen, V.L. *Psychological Factors in Poverty.* Chicago: Markham, 1970.

Almaguer, T. "Toward a Study of Chicano Colonialism." *Aztlán: Chicano Journal of the Social Sciences and the Arts* 2, no. 1 (Spring, 1971): 7-22.

Barrera, M. *Race and Class in the Southwest, A Theory of Racial Inequality.* Notre Dame: University of Notre Dame Press, 1979.

Beebe, R. *Spanish Influence in the American Tradition: A Selected Bibliography.* Washington, D.C.: Library of Congress, Legislative Reference Service, 1964.

Bettelheim, B., and M.B. Janowitz. *The Dynamics of Prejudice.* New York: Harper and Brothers, 1950.

Blanco-Aguinago, C. "El laberinto fabricado por Octavio Paz." *Aztlán: Chicano Journal of the Social Sciences and the Arts* 3, no. 1 (Spring, 1972): 1-12.

Borah, W. "Race and Class in Mexico." *Pacific Historical Review* 23 (1954).

Brown, I. *Understanding Other Cultures.* Englewood Cliffs, New Jersey: Prentice Hall, 1963.

Brown, R. McA. *Religion and Violence.* Philadelphia: The Westminster Press, 1973.

Burling, R. *Man's Many Voices: Language in Its Cultural Context.* New York: Holt, Rinehart, Winston, 1970.

Burma, J.H., ed. *Mexican Americans in the United States.* Cambridge, Mass.: Schenkman, 1970.

Cabrera, Y.A. "A Study of American and Mexican-American Culture Values and Their Significance in Education." *Dissertation Abstracts* 25 (1964): 309.

Carter, T.P. "The Negative Self-concept of Mexican American Students." *School and Society* 96 (1968): 207-209.

Cortés, C.E. "The Anthropology and Sociology of the Mexican-Americans: The

Distortion of Mexican-American History (A Review Essay)." *El Grito* 2, no. 1 (Fall, 1968): 13-26.

DeBlassie, R.R. *Counseling with Mexican American Youth: Preconceptions and Processes.* Austin: Learning Concepts, Inc., 1976.

Díaz-Guerrero, R. *Psychology of the Mexican: Culture and Personality.* Austin: University of Texas Press, 1975.

Dufrenne, M. *La personnalité de base.* Paris: Presses Universitaires de France, 1953.

Duran, R. *Salubridad Chicana: Su Preservación y Mantenimiento: The Chicano Plan for Mental Health.* Denver, 1975.

Dworkin, A. G. "Stereotypes and Self-images Held by Native-born and Foreign-born Mexican-Americans." *Sociology and Social Research* 49, no. 2 (1965): 214-224.

Frazier, F. *Race and Culture Contacts in the Modern World.* New York, 1957.

Freire, P. *The Pedagogy of the Oppressed.* New York: Herder and Herder, 1970.

Hall, Edward T. *The Silent Language.* New York: Fawcett Premier, 1965.

Helm, J., ed. *Spanish Speaking People in the United States.* Proceedings of the Meeting of the American Ethnological Society. Seattle: University of Washington, 1968.

Hernandez, D. *Mexican American Challenge to a Sacred Cow.* Los Angeles: Aztlán Publications, 1970.

Hewes, G. "The Mexican in Search of 'the Mexican.' " *American Journal of Economics and Sociology* 18 (Jan. 1954): 109-223.

Hoetink, H. "Colonial Psychology and Race." *Journal of Economic History* 21 (1961).

Humphrey, N.D. "The Stereotype and the Social Types of Mexican-American Youths." *Journal of Social Psychology* 22, no. 1 (1945): 69-78.

Krickus, R. *Pursuing the American Dream.* New York: Anchor Books, 1976.

Limón, J.E. "Stereotyping and Chicano Resistance." *Aztlán: Chicano Journal of the Social Sciences and the Arts* 4, no. 2 (Fall, 1973): 257-270.

Lowrie, S.H. *Culture Conflict in Texas, 1821-1835.* New York: AMS Press, 1967.

Luria, A.R. *Nature of Human Conflicts.* New York: Liveright, 1932.

Martinez, T.M. "Advertising and racism: The case of the Mexican American." *El Grito* 2, no. 3 (1969): 3-13.

Memmi, A. *The Colonizer and the Colonized.* Boston: Beacon Press, 1972.

Morin, R. *Among the Valiant.* California: Borden, 1966.

Novak, M. *The Rise of the Unmeltable Ethnics: Politics and Culture in the Seventies.* New York: Macmillan, 1971.

Ortega, P.O. *We Are Chicanos.* New York: Washington Square Press, 1973.

Paz, O. "Eroticism and Gastrosophy." *Daedalus* 101, no. 4 (Fall, 1972): 67-86.

———. *The Labyrinth of Solitude.* New York: Grove Press, 1961.

Peck, R.F., and R. Díaz-Guerrero. "The Meaning of Love in Mexico and the United States." *American Psychologist* 17 (1962): 329.

Powell, P.W. *Tree of Hate: Propaganda and Prejudices Affecting United States Relations with the Hispanic World.* New York: Basic Books, Inc., 1971.

Rainwater, L. *What Money Buys: Inequality and the Social Meaning of Income.* Washington: The Library of Urban Affairs, 1976.

Ricard, R. *The Spiritual Conquest of Mexico.* Berkeley: University of California Press, 1966.

Rocco, R.A. "The Chicano in the Social Sciences: Traditional Concepts, Myths and Images." *Atzlán: Chicano Journal of the Social Sciences and the Arts* 1, no. 2 (Fall, 1970).

Rodríguez, D.E. "Some Psychological and Educational Aspects of Bilingualism." *Aztlán: Chicano Journal of the Social Sciences and the Arts* 12, no. 1 (Spring, 1971): 79-106.

Romanell, P. *Making of the Mexican Mind.* Notre Dame: University of Notre Dame Press, 1952.

Romano, O.I. "Donship in a Mexican-American Community in Texas." *American Anthropologist* 62, no. 6 (1960): 966-976.

———. "The Historical and Intellectual Presence of Mexican Americans." *El Grito* (Winter, 1969): 39-40.

———. "Social Science, Objectivity and the Chicanos." *El Grito* 4, no. 1 (Fall, 1970): 4-16.

Romero, J., and M. Sandoval. *Reluctant Dawn.* San Antonio: Mexican-American Cultural Center, 1977.

Ruffie, J. *De la Biologie a la Culture.* Paris: Flammarion, 1976.

Ryan, W. *Blaming the Victim.* New York: Image Books, 1972.

Samora, J., and P.V. Simon. *A History of the Mexican-American People.* Notre Dame: University of Notre Dame Press, 1977.

Sánchez, E. *Salubridad Chicana: Su Preservación y Mantenimiento: The Chicano Plan for Mental Health.* Denver, 1975.

Simmons, O.G. "The Mutual Images and Expectations of Anglo-Americans and Mexican-Americans." *Daedalus* 90, no. 2 (1961): 286-299.

Smith, A. *Transracial Communication, U.S.A.* Englewood, New Jersey: Prentice Hall, 1973.

Stevens Arroyo, A.M. *Prophets Denied Honor: An Anthology on the Hispanic Church in the United States.* Maryknoll, New York: Orbis, 1980.

Turner, P.R. *Bilingualism in the Southwest.* Arizona: The University of Arizona Press, 1975.

de Unamuno, M. *Del sentimiento tragico de la vida.* New York: Las Americas Publishing Co.

Wagner, N., and M.J. Haug. *Chicanos: Social and Psychological Perspectives.* St. Louis: Mosby, 1977.

Waters, F. *Mexico Mystique.* Chicago: Swallow Press, Inc., 1975.

Theological

Alfaro, J. *Jesus, the Light of the World: The Gospel of St. John.* San Antonio: Mexican-American Cultural Center, 1977.

Audinet, J. "Agir pastoral et révélation." J. Audinet et al. *Révélation de dieu et language des hommes.* Paris: Cerf, 1972.

———. "Questions de methode." *Le point théologique* 1 (1970): 73-93.

———. "Théologie pratique et pratique théologique." *Le point théologique* 21 (1977).

Bammel, E. *The Trial of Jesus.* Chicago: Allenson, 1970.

Baum, G. *Religion and Alienation.* New York: Paulist, 1975.

Boff, L. *Jesus Christ Liberator.* Maryknoll, New York: Orbis, 1978.

Boobyer, G.H. "Galilee and Galilean in St. Mark's Gospel." *The Bulletin of the John Rylands Library* 35 (1953): 334-448.

Bornkamm, G. *Jesus of Nazareth.* New York: Harper and Row, 1960.

Bourgeois, H. *Libérer Jésus—cristologies actuelles.* Paris: Le Centurion, 1977.

Brown, R. *The Birth of the Messiah.* New York: Doubleday, 1977.

———. *The Gospel According to John.* Anchor Bible, vols. 29 and 29a. Garden City, New York: Doubleday, 1966.

van Cangh, J.M. "La Galilee dans l'evangile de Marc: un lieu théologique?" *Revue Biblique* 79, no. 1 (1972): 59-76.

Chenu, M.D. "L'Eglise des pauvres á Vatican II." *Concilium* 124 (1977).

Clevenot, M. *Approches matérialistes de la Bible.* Paris: Cerf, 1976.

Comblin, J. *Jesus of Nazareth.* Maryknoll, New York: Orbis, 1976.

———. *Teología de la misión.* Buenos Aires: Latinoamerica Libros, 1977.

Cross, F.L. *The Early Christian Fathers*. London, 1960.

Danielou, J. "Comment dialoguer avec les culture non-chrétiennes?" *L'encontro cristiano con le culture*. Milano: Vita e pensiero, 1965.

Davies, W.D. *The Gospel and the Land*. Berkeley: University of California Press, 1974.

————. *The Setting of the Sermon on the Mount*. Cambridge University Press, 1963.

Díaz-Merino, L. "Galilea en el IV Evangelio." *Estudios Bíblicos* 31, no. 3 (July-Sept., 1972): 247-274.

Dideberg, D., and P.M. Beernaert. "Jésus vint en Galilée: Essai sur la structure de Marc 1:21-45." *Nouvelle Revue Theologique* 98 (April, 1976): 306-323.

Dupont, J. *Les Beatitúdes*. Paris: Gabalda, 1969.

————. "La premiére Pentecôte chrétienne: Etudes sur les Actes." *Lectio Divina* 45 (1967): 481-502.

Duquoc, C. *Dimensions of Spirituality*. New York: Herder and Herder, 1970.

————. *Jésus, Hombre Libre*. Salamanca: Sígueme, 1975.

Edersheim, A. *The Life and Times of Jesus the Messiah*. Grand Rapids, Michigan: Eerdmans, 1954.

Elizondo, E., and J. Linskens. "Pentecost and Pluralism." *Momentum* (October, 1975).

Elizondo, V. *La Morenita, Evangelizer of the Americas*. San Antonio: Mexican-American Cultural Center, 1980.

Ellacuria, I. *Freedom Made Flesh. The Mission of Christ and His Church*. Maryknoll, New York: Orbis, 1976.

Elliott-Binns, L.E. *Galilean Christianity. Studies in Biblical Theology* 16. London: SCM Press, 1956.

Ford, J.M. "Social Consciousness in the New Testament: Jesus and Paul—a Contrast." *New Blackfriars* 57, no. 673 (1976): 244-254.

France, R.T. *I Came to Set the Earth on Fire: A Portrait of Jesus*. Downers Grove, Illinois: InterVarsity, 1976.

Galilea, S. *Following Jesus*. Maryknoll, New York: Orbis, 1981.

Geffré, C. *A New Age in Theology*. New York: Paulist, 1974.

———— and G. Gutiérrez. *The Mystical and Political Dimension of the Christian Faith. Concilium* 96. New York: Herder and Herder, 1974.

Girard, R. *Des Choses Cachées depuis la fondation du monde*. Paris: Bernard Grasset, 1978.

Gonzales-Faus, J.I. *La humanidad nueva—ensayo de cristologia*. Madrid: EAPSA, 1975.

————. *Acceso a Jesus*. Salamanca: Sígueme, 1979.

Gutiérrez, G. *A Theology of Liberation: History, Politics and Salvation*. Maryknoll, New York: Orbis, 1973.

————. *El Dios de la Vida*. Lima, Peru: Pontificia Universidad Católica, 1980.

Hendrickx, H. *The Infancy Narratives*. Manila: East Asian Pastoral Institute, 1975.

Jaeger, W. *Early Christianity and Greek Paideia*. New York: Oxford University Press, 1961.

Jeremias, J. *Jerusalem au temps de Jésus*. Paris: Cerf, 1967.

Juster, J. *Les Juifs dans l'empire romain*. Paris, 1914.

Kannengiesser, C. "Avenir des traditions fondatrices." *Recherches de science religieuse* 65, no. 1 (1977): 139-168.

————. *Foi en la resurrection—resurrection de la foi*. Paris: Beuschesne, 1976.

Keck, L.E. "The Historical Jesus and Christology." *Perkins Journal* 29, no. 3 (1976): 14-26.

Kraft, C.H. *Christianity in Culture*. Maryknoll, New York: Orbis, 1979.

Kung, H. *On Being a Christian*. Garden City, New York: Doubleday, 1976.

Lagasse, S. *Jesus et l'enfant*. Paris: Lecoffre, 1969.

Lagrange, M.J. *Le judaisme avant Jésus-Christ*. Paris, 1931.

Lane, D. *The Reality of Jesus*. New York: Paulist Press, 1975.

Laurentin, R. *Luc 1-11*. Paris: Lecoffre, 1964.

Lightfoot, R.H. *Locality and Doctrine in the Gospel*. New York, 1938.

Linskens, J. *Christ, the Liberator of the Poor*. San Antonio: Mexican-American Cultural Center, 1976.

———. *The Foundational Experience of the Early Christian Movement*. Manila: East Asian Pastoral Institute, 1977.

———. *The Meaning of Christian Pentecost*. San Antonio: Mexican-American Cultural Center, 1975.

Livio, J.B. "Histoire de la Galilee." *Bible et Terre Sainte* 183 (1976): 9-10.

Lohmeyer, E. *Galilea und Jerusalem*. Göttingen: Vandenhoeck and Ruprecht. 1936.

Lucas, I. *The Browning of America, The Hispanic Revolution in the American Church*. Chicago: Fides Claretian, 1981.

Mackey, J.P. *Jesus, the Man and the Myth*. New York: Paulist Press, 1979.

Marstin, R. *Beyond Our Tribal Gods: The Maturing of Faith*. Maryknoll, New York: Orbis, 1979.

Matasunaga, K. "The Galileans in the Fourth Gospel." *Annals of the Japanese Biblical Institute* (1976): 139-158.

Meeks, W. "Galilee and Judea in the Fourth Gospel." *Journal of Biblical Literature* 85, no. 2 (1966): 159-169.

Metz, J. *Theology of the World*. New York: Herder and Herder, 1969.

———. *Faith in History & Society, Toward a Practical Fundamental Theology*. New York: The Seabury Press, 1980.

Meyers, F. "Galilean Regionalism as a Factor in Historical Reconstruction." *Bulletin of the American Schools of Oriental Research* 221 (1976): 93-101.

Perrin, N. *Jesus and the Language of the Kingdom: Symbol and Metaphor in New Testament Interpretation*. Philadelphia: Fortress Press, 1976.

———. *Rediscovering the Teachings of Jesus*. New York: Harper and Row, 1976.

Ramirez, R. *Fiesta, Worship and Family*. San Antonio: Mexican-American Cultural Center, 1981.

Raschke, C.A. "Hermeneutics as Historical Process: Discourse, Text, and the Revolution of Symbols." *Journal of the American Academy of Religion* 35, no. 1 (March, 1977): 74-75.

Richardson, C.C. *Early Christian Fathers*. New York: Macmillan, 1970.

Samain, E. "Le récit lucanien du voyage de Jésus vers Jerusalem." *Foi et Vie: Cahiers bibliques* 12 (1973).

———. "Le récit de Pentecôte (Actes 2:1-13)." *Foi et Vie: Cahiers bibliques* 10 (1971).

Sapin, J. "Aspects de la Galilee." *Bible et Terre Sainte* 183 (1976): 2-8.

Schlierse, F.J. *Jesus von Nazaret*. Mainz, 1972.

Schreiter, R. "Christology in the Jewish-Christian Encounter." *Journal of the American Academy of Religion* 34, no. 4 (Dec. 1976): 693-703.

Schubert, K. *Jésus a lumiére de Judaïsme du premier siécle*. Paris: Cerf, 1974.

Schurer, E. *The History of the Jewish People in the Age of Jesus Christ (175 B.C.- A.D. 135)*. Revised and edited by G. Vermes and F. Millar. Cf. *New Testament Abstracts* 18 (1976): 260.

Schillebeeckx, E. *Jesus: An Experiment in Christology*. New York: Seabury, 1979.

———. *Christ: The Experience of Jesus as Lord*. New York: Seabury, 1980.

Sleeper, C.F. "Pentecost and Resurrection." *Journal of Biblical Literature* 84 (1965): 389-399.

Smulders, P. *The Fathers on Christology*. De Pere, Wisconsin: St. Norbert Abbey Press, 1968.

Starr, C.G. *Civilization and the Caesars: The Intellectual Revolution in the Roman Empire*. Ithaca, New York, 1955.

Tillard, J.M.R. *Foi populaire, foi savante*. Paris: Cerf, 1976.

Tillich, P. *Theology of Culture*. New York: Oxford University Press, 1969.

Torres, S., and J. Eagleson, eds. "The Latin American Theologians." *Theology in the Americas*. Maryknoll, New York: Orbis, 1976.

Vawter, B. *This Man Jesus: An Essay toward a New Testament Christology*. Garden City, New York: Doubleday, 1973.

Vermes, G. *Jesus the Jew: A Historian's Reading of the Gospels.*. New York: Macmillan, 1974.

Weiss, J. *The History of Primitive Christianity*. Completed by R. Knopf and edited by F.C. Grant. New York, 1937.

SCRIPTURE INDEX

GENERAL INDEX

72; as Galilean, fulfilling the prophetic vocation, 55; having to die because of his exposure of the establishment, 74-75; in-out of Jewish society, 107; questioning deification of structures, 60, 66; sending a new spirit to judge all structures, 66; as suffering servant, 75

Jesus Christ, as rabbi, 60; reaffirming tradition, 66; refusing to reject or condemn, 75; as rejected by his own people, 66

Jesus Christ, and resurrection, 79; beyond categories of time and space, 79; as continuity with earthly Jesus, 79; at core of faith, 79; as discontinuity, 79, 88; giving meaning tò the Nazareth-to-Jerusalem process, 75; illuminating way of the earthly Jesus, 80-81; as liberation of the powerless, 117; and new life in the Risen Lord, 79; as new movement, 79; as paradox of death-life, 115; revealing sovereignty of God-Father over all, 79; as source of joyful proclamation, 115

Jesus Christ, temptations of, 59, 72; as refusal to use magic, 71

Jesus Christ, as "the Way," 45, 68, 107; alternative to merely human ways, 88; assuming the condition of a slave, 91; astonished Emperor Julian, 80; clearer in Resurrection faith, 80-81; demanding fidelity to the Jerusalem mission, 105; demanding nonconformity to the ways of the world, 104-105; from Galilee to Jerusalem, 103-105; in Greco-Roman soil, 84; as identity and mission of his followers, 116; as incarnation-transcendence, 124; as invitation to following of the Cross, 72; from Nazareth to Jerusalem as liberation, 80-81; not understood by disciples, 72; offering radical newness, 119; open to all, 85; opposite to way of Pharisees, Scribes, and priests, 72; in the persecuted Galilean Church, 113; possible through the Spirit crying "Abba" within, 80; as radical forgiveness, 120; as struggle against evil, 72; transcending the dilemma of acceptance-rejection, 61; understood only after resurrection, 115

Jews, 7; as dominating culturally, 86; as a people, 98; as threatened by the dominant society, 98

John Paul II, 93

Juan Diego, 11, 45, 123

Kannenguser, Charles, S.J., 3

Kennedy, John F., 29, 39

King, Martin Luther, 105

Kingdom, 53, 71, 72; as achieving intimacy for the Father's children, 62-63; as both continuity and transcendence, 66; as celebrated by Mexican-Americans, 102; of God's grace, not vengeance, 56-57; as interdependence of cultures and races, 64; as new basis for society, 64; not apocalyptic end, but beginning, 56; open to rejected, 57; proclaimed in mestizo celebrations, 124; realized in table fellowship, 65, 70; as revelation of the human person and of God, 54; as salvation and liberation, 66; symbolized by Galilee, 66; understood as solely for the chosen people, 65; as universal acceptance, 53

Kittel, 50

Lane, Dermot A., 79, 127

Language, as a problem, 27

Law, learned by Jesus the Jew, 54; as "magic," 71

Liberal capitalism, 111, 112

Liberation movements, 19

Liberation, 53, 105, 115; as confrontation with injustice, 103, 112; from egotism by the way of Jesus, 88; experienced in fiesta, 122; and the followers of Jesus, 58; from the god-making process, 86; and God's election as not a privilege to be passive, 105; through the Gospel, 118; through the power of transformed suffering, 100; proclaimed in popular celebrations, 102; requiring the Mexican-American to face limitations, 109; through the resurrection, 116; for self-determination and new creation, 100; as transforming and transcending the evils of an oppressor society, 103; as true freedom of the children of God, 66

Lightfoot, R.H., 49, 127

Linskens, John, 3

Lohmeyer, E., 50, 127

Manifest destiny, 14

Westminster United Presbyterian Church
1501 WEST CLEVELAND RD.
SOUTH BEND, INDIANA 46628